Folens
History in Action 4

Author:
Karen Cooksey

Acknowledgements

The author and publishers would like to thank the following for permission to reproduce the following copyright material:

p.18 Extract taken from: http://www.bbc.co.uk/history/ancient/egyptians.
p.19 Illustration based on a wall painting from the tomb of Nebamun, held by The British Museum.
pp.33 and 35 Extracts taken from *The Complete Sagas of Icelanders*, trans. Bernard Scudder (Reykjavik: Leifur Eiriksson, 1997).
pp.65, 66, 75 (left) Imperial War Museum, London.
p.65 Extract taken from *The Home Front: Prisoners of War* by Fiona Reynoldson. Reproduced by permission of Hodder and Stoughton Limited.
p.66 Extract taken from the papers of Miss J B Male. This collection is held in the Department of Documents at the Imperial War Museum. Every effort has been made to contact the copyright holders but this has not been possible.
p.69 Extract taken from PROJECT HOMEWORK: WORLD WAR II by Hazel Poole, first published in the UK by Franklin Watts in 1994, a division of the Watts Publishing Group Limited, 96 Leonard Street, London EC2A 4XD.
p.78 Transcript taken from an interview with Cynthia Montreal.

© 2005 Folens Limited, on behalf of the author.

United Kingdom: Folens Publishers, Apex Business Centre, Boscombe Road, Dunstable, LU5 4RL.
Email: folens@folens.com

Ireland: Folens Publishers, Greenhills Road, Tallaght, Dublin 24.
Email: info@folens.ie

Poland: JUKA, ul. Renesansowa 38, Warsaw 01-905.

Commissioning editor: Zoë Nichols
Editor: Caroline Marmo
Layout artist: Patricia Hollingsworth
Illustrations: Mark Stacey and Mike Lacey (pages 14 and 17)
Cover image: © Hulton-Deutsch Collection/CORBIS
Cover design: Philippa Jarvis

First published 2005 by Folens Limited.

Every effort has been made to contact copyright holders of material used in this publication. If any copyright holder has been overlooked, we should be pleased to make any necessary arrangements.

British Library Cataloguing in Publication Data. A catalogue record for this publication is available from the British Library.

ISBN 1 84303 679 7

Contents

Introduction

Folens History in Action meets the requirements for the National Curriculum in England and Wales, and is compatible with the schemes of work published in England by the Qualifications and Curriculum Authority (QCA). It will work best when combined with a range of history resources such as books, photos, videos, artefacts and, for some topics, interviews with visitors.

Aims of Folens History in Action

The overall aim of the book is that children should: develop knowledge and understanding of significant periods, people and events in history; and learn to interpret historical evidence and understand that knowledge about history is subject to interpretation.

The aim of individual activities is to provide opportunities for children to engage with the subject matter and process it in some way, such as matching, sequencing, using information to draw, write a specific form of text, or label a diagram. Children's thinking skills will develop better if they are allowed to verbalise their thought processes in pairs or small groups; most of the activities are designed to be used in this way.

The Structure of Folens History in Action

The book is divided into four units, each covering a history topic suitable for Year 3 and Year 4, as defined by the schemes of work. Each unit contains a term's work; it is expected that teachers will choose three of the topics for the year.

After an initial introduction to the River Nile and its connection to the farming year, the unit on **Ancient Eygpt** provides opportunities for children to examine this civilization through remains: models, carvings, paintings and written evidence. The following unit, **Vikings**, also places emphasis on different types of evidence, and encourages children to compare them for reliability. It also covers the origin of the Vikings and aspects of their way of life as invaders, settlers, farmers, raiders and explorers. The unit on **Henry VIII** begins with the Tudor family, Henry VIII's personality, abilities and appearance and his role as king. It then focuses on the six marriages: how and why they began and ended. The first activities in **World War Two** will help children to learn how and when the war began, and the main personalities and countries involved. The remaining activities, with the exception of one (about Anne Frank), deal with the effect of the war on people in Britain, and include the experiences of children.

The units are further divided into sub-topics, each starting with a teachers' page. The teachers' page contains notes to explain and provide background for the activity sheets which follow.

---

gives the objectives covered in the activity sheets

gives a brief introduction to the topic and information relevant to the activities

suggests a useful way in which teachers can prepare the class for each activity

brief notes on how to deliver the activity which forms the main part of the lesson, and which the majority of children will complete

a suggestion as to how to make the activity suitable for children at a lower level of achievement

an idea for a more challenging activity which can be given to higher achieving or enthusiastic children after they have completed the main activity

an idea for rounding up and consolidating the learning after all the activities referred to on the teachers' page have been completed

Ancient Egypt

Learning Objective

Children should:
■ understand the importance of the River Nile for the Ancient Egyptians.

Background

The Ancient Egyptian civilization spans a period of about 3000 years. It begins with the earliest written records in hieroglyphics at around 3100BC, and declines with the occupation of Egypt by the Greeks in 332BC and then by the Romans in 30BC. This civilisation would not have existed without the Nile. In Egypt's desert climate the river provided almost all the water. The annual floods left a rich alluvial soil where crops were grown. The soil was so fertile that enough food for everyone could be grown by farmers, thus freeing up other sections of the population to be craft workers, administrators or scribes.

The river defined the seasons in the following way: 'Inundation', from July to October, when the land was flooded; 'Emergence', from November to March, when the land reappeared and ploughing and planting could begin; and 'Heat', from March to May, when the crops were harvested. The river also provided fish, the main source of animal protein. Away from the banks of the Nile the landscape was desert. Wheels would sink in the sandy soil, so boats were the most useful form of transport. Due to their dependence on the river, the Ancient Egyptians lived along the banks of the Nile and in the Nile delta, a pattern of settlement that still exists today.

▲ Starting Points	▼ Main Activity	Simplified Activity	Extension Activity
E1 *'The River Nile'* Show Egypt on a world map and place Ancient Egypt on a timeline. Explain the importance of the Nile for the Ancient Egyptians.	Make sure that the children understand what the pictures represent before asking them to write the explanations.	Ask the children to write one sentence for each picture. Provide some word clues to help them.	Give the children atlases and ask them to find out where most people in Egypt live today. Is it still near the Nile?
E2 *'The Ancient Egyptian farming year'* Explain that the Ancient Egyptians grew all of their own food and talk about what this involves: ploughing, planting/ sowing, irrigating, harvesting and storing.	Read the paragraph with the children and discuss any new vocabulary or concepts. Make sure that they understand what the diagram should show.	Give the children a copy of the sheet with the diagram partially filled in and ask them to complete it.	Ask the children to imagine either a good year or a bad year for an Ancient Egyptian farmer and to write his or her account.

Plenary ◄

Recap with a word association game. Write 'The River Nile' on the board. Give some examples of associated words (*irrigation*, *crop*, *desert*). Divide the class into teams. The team that thinks of the most words (and can explain the connections) is the winner.

Ancient Egypt

Learning Objective

Children should:
- understand the importance of the River Nile for the Ancient Egyptians.

Background

The Ancient Egyptian civilization spans a period of about 3000 years. It begins with the earliest written records in hieroglyphics at around 3100BC, and declines with the occupation of Egypt by the Greeks in 332BC and then by the Romans in 30BC. This civilisation would not have existed without the Nile. In Egypt's desert climate the river provided almost all the water. The annual floods left a rich alluvial soil where crops were grown. The soil was so fertile that enough food for everyone could be grown by farmers, thus freeing up other sections of the population to be craft workers, administrators or scribes.

The river defined the seasons in the following way: 'Inundation', from July to October, when the land was flooded; 'Emergence', from November to March, when the land reappeared and ploughing and planting could begin; and 'Heat', from March to May, when the crops were harvested. The river also provided fish, the main source of animal protein. Away from the banks of the Nile the landscape was desert. Wheels would sink in the sandy soil, so boats were the most useful form of transport. Due to their dependence on the river, the Ancient Egyptians lived along the banks of the Nile and in the Nile delta, a pattern of settlement that still exists today.

Starting Points	Main Activity	Simplified Activity	Extension Activity
E1 *'The River Nile'* Show Egypt on a world map and place Ancient Egypt on a timeline. Explain the importance of the Nile for the Ancient Egyptians.	Make sure that the children understand what the pictures represent before asking them to write the explanations.	Ask the children to write one sentence for each picture. Provide some word clues to help them.	Give the children atlases and ask them to find out where most people in Egypt live today. Is it still near the Nile?
E2 *'The Ancient Egyptian farming year'* Explain that the Ancient Egyptians grew all of their own food and talk about what this involves: ploughing, planting/ sowing, irrigating, harvesting and storing.	Read the paragraph with the children and discuss any new vocabulary or concepts. Make sure that they understand what the diagram should show.	Give the children a copy of the sheet with the diagram partially filled in and ask them to complete it.	Ask the children to imagine either a good year or a bad year for an Ancient Egyptian farmer and to write his or her account.

Plenary

Recap with a word association game. Write 'The River Nile' on the board. Give some examples of associated words (*irrigation, crop, desert*). Divide the class into teams. The team that thinks of the most words (and can explain the connections) is the winner.

The River Nile

- Use the picture clues to help you explain how important the Nile was for the Ancient Egyptians.

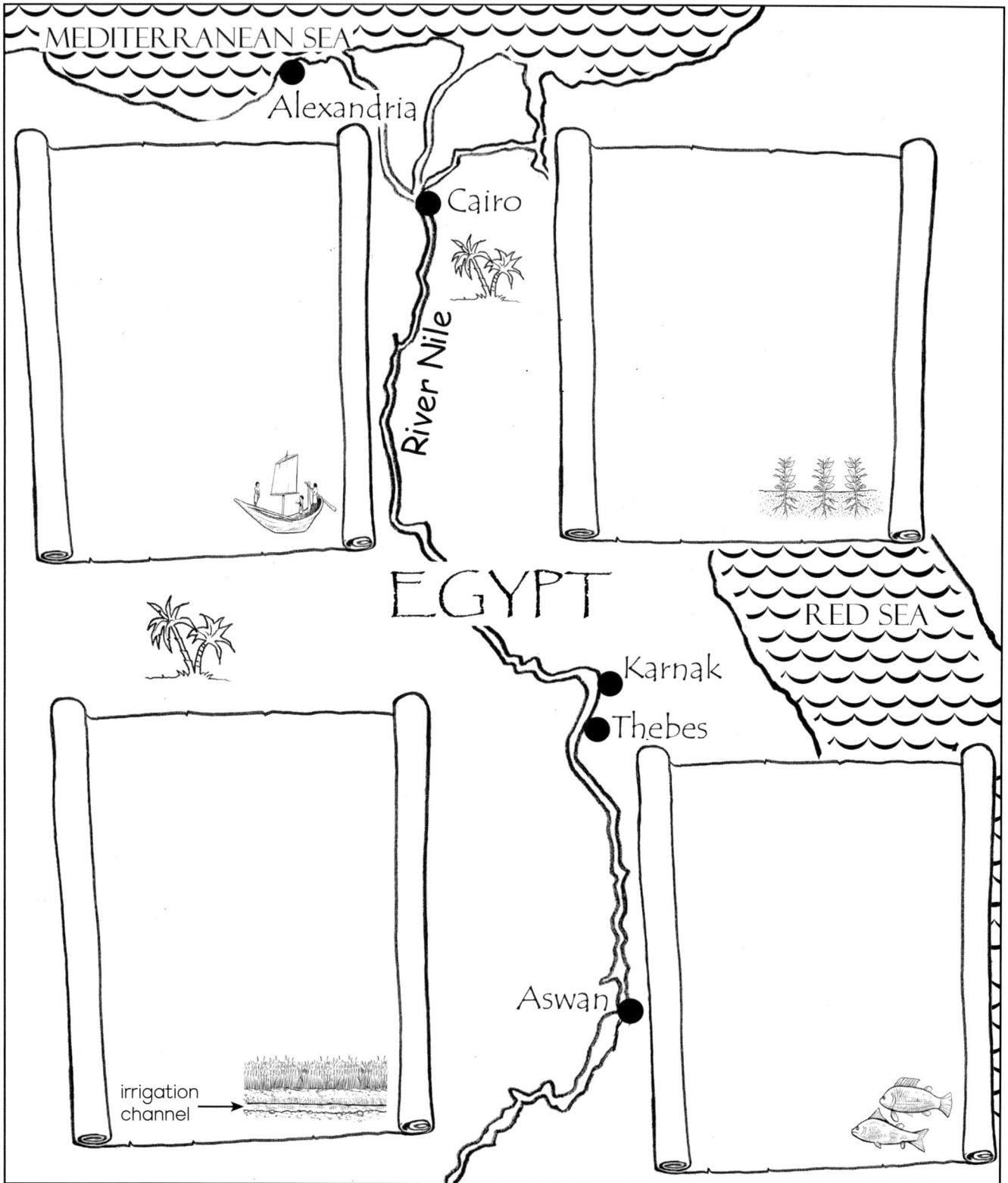

MEDITERRANEAN SEA

Alexandria

Cairo

River Nile

EGYPT

RED SEA

Karnak

Thebes

irrigation channel

Aswan

- Describe the climate of Egypt.

_____

_____

FOLENS HISTORY IN ACTION 4

The Ancient Egyptian farming year

- Use three colours on the diagram below to show the yearly cycle for the Ancient Egyptian farmers. Label the three sections with the names of the seasons: **Inundation**, **Emergence** and **Heat**. Draw the crops in the correct sections.

The year was divided into three seasons. It began in July when the waters of the River Nile started to rise. In October, the water fell, leaving a rich black soil. The farmers ploughed the soil and planted wheat, barley or flax. They dug channels and filled them with water to irrigate the crops. The crops grew and ripened. March to May was the harvest time. Some of the grain was saved for seed; some was paid to the landowner; some the farmer kept and stored. Before the next flood, farmers built banks to help spread the floodwater across the fields.

Vegetables could be grown all year but they had to be watered regularly. Dates, on the other hand, didn't need any watering because the date palm has long roots that can get water from deep in the soil. The dates were harvested in September or October.

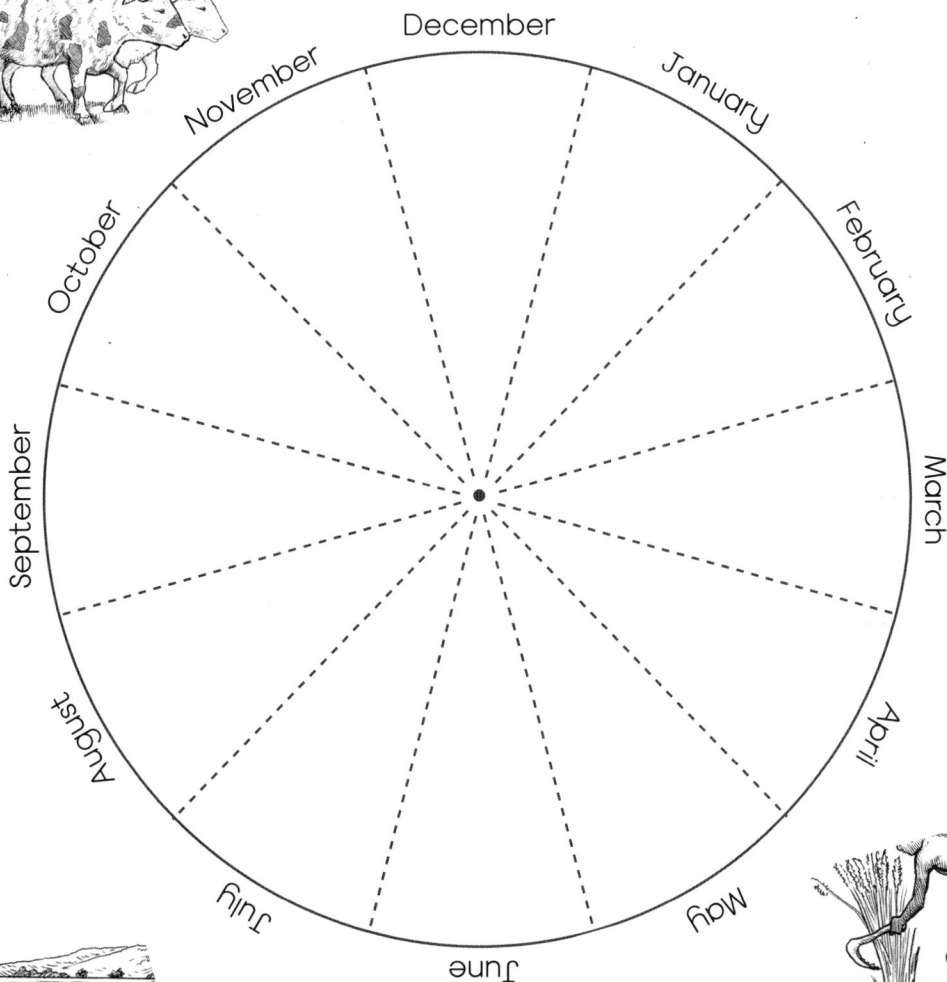

Children should:

- know the connection between tombs and pyramids, and the beliefs of the Ancient Egyptians.
- understand why we have so much evidence of the Ancient Egyptian civilisation.

Background

The Ancient Egyptians believed that a dead person's soul travelled to the underworld, passed through trials and ordeals, including the weighing of their heart against a feather, and (if the heart was not too heavy) finally reached the afterlife. Wealthy Egyptians were buried with everything they would need for the journey: a guide to the underworld in the form of a scroll of papers (the *Book of the Dead*) and spells inscribed on the walls; food; furniture; and models and paintings of all aspects of the person's life, which would transform into the real thing in the afterlife. Bodies were mummified because without them the dead would not be able to progress in the underworld. The pharaohs were different; they were already divine, so after death they would join the other gods. Poor people were buried in simple holes in hot sand, or small tombs cut into the ground.

Most tombs and pyramids lost their valuable contents to grave robbers. The tomb of Tutankhamun was relatively small but rare in never having been entered. The wealth of contents indicates what might have been found in grander burial chambers. Much more is known about the wealthy Egyptians whose tombs and temples were built in the desert, than about the majority whose houses have been washed away by the floodwaters of the Nile. Even though so much has been lost, compared to other civilisations of the time, we have a relatively accurate picture of how the Ancient Egyptians lived. This is also due to the dry climate.

Starting Points	Main Activity	Simplified Activity	Extension Activity
E3 *'The afterlife'* Explain what Ancient Egyptians believed about the afterlife.	Ask the children to look at the pictures in pairs and to recall as much as they can about each of the objects before writing about them.	Give the children a list of sentences, such as 'a guide to the underworld' that they can match to the pictures.	Ask the children to write an imaginative account of the discovery of an Ancient Egyptian burial chamber.
E4 *'Sealing the tomb'* Explain that robbery was a serious problem in Ancient Egypt and that tombs had to be 'sealed'.	Ask the children to work in twos or threes and imagine that they are the workers who have been left to seal the tomb. Give them time to solve the problem before discussing the solution as a class and asking them to write an explanation.	After they have discussed the problem, give the children some written questions that will help them to describe the solution. (*Where did you position yourself? How did you slide the blocks?*)	Give the children a range of resources and ask them to find out how successful the sealing of tombs was. (*How many pyramids have been found with all the contents still there?*) Then ask them to report to the class.
E5 *'Evidence from Ancient Egypt'* Talk about the things that have helped and hindered the study of Ancient Egypt.	Ask the children to discuss the nine factors at the top of the page in pairs, before carrying out the written task.	Ask the children to cut out the nine factors and stick them under the correct heading.	Ask the children to write part two of their imaginative account, describing ways to preserve the information (i.e. not moving finds, contacting archaeologists).

Plenary

Draw a pyramid on the board and ask the children to use a mixture of knowledge and imagination to tell 'the story of the pyramid'. *Why was it built? Who for? What went inside? What happened to these things?*

The afterlife

● Explain how these things would help an Ancient Egyptian to make the journey through the underworld to the afterlife.

wall painting

_____

_____

_____

_____

_____

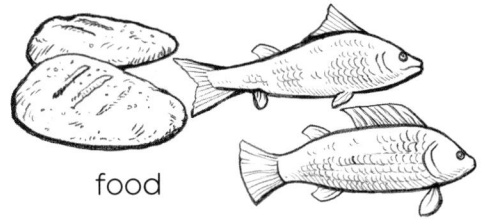

food

_____

_____

_____

_____

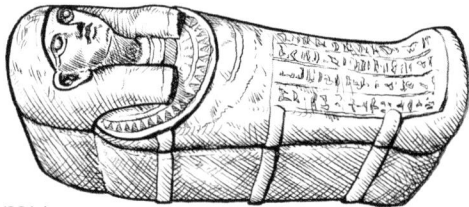

mummy

_____

_____

_____

_____

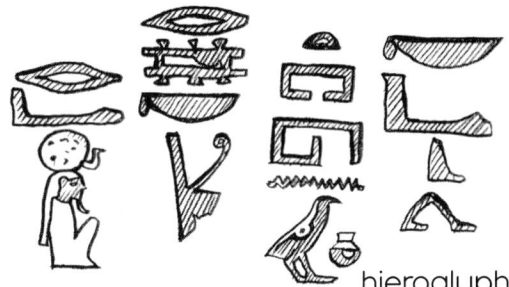

hieroglyphics

_____

_____

_____

_____

model boat

_____

_____

_____

Book of the Dead

_____

_____

_____

Sealing the tomb

The pharaoh has been buried with all his treasures. You are one of the workmen who have been left inside the Great Gallery to seal it. You must block all entrances to the chambers with stone and then get out. You cannot crawl up an air shaft.

- Study the diagram and work out how you are going to do it and get out alive!
- Draw your escape route and where you will put the stone blocks. Remember to seal your final entrance.

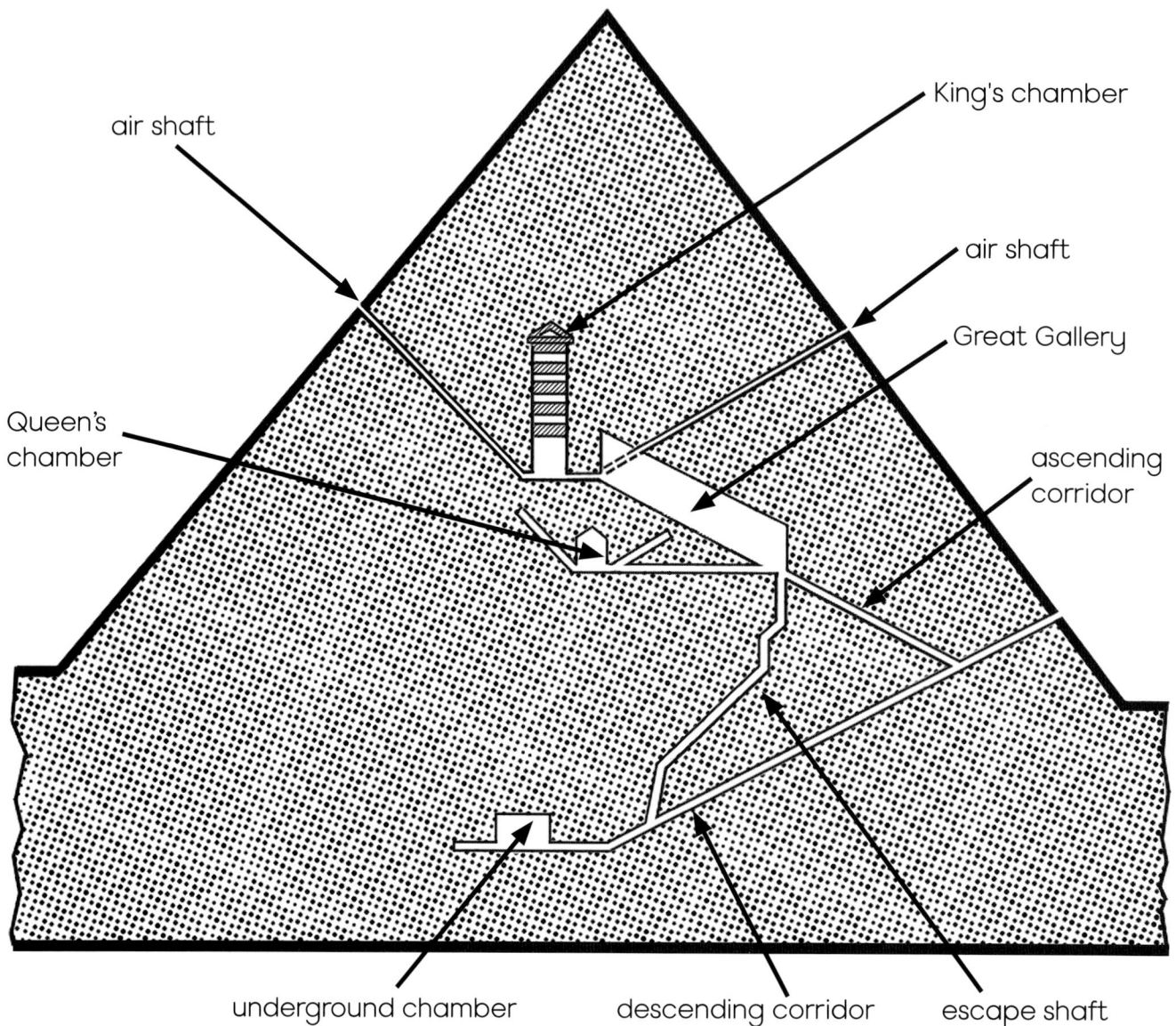

air shaft

King's chamber

air shaft

Great Gallery

Queen's chamber

ascending corridor

underground chamber   descending corridor   escape shaft

- You are out in the fresh air! Explain how you did it.

_____

_____

_____

_____

FOLENS HISTORY IN ACTION 4 © Folens (copiable page)

Evidence from Ancient Egypt

● Write these things under the correct headings below. Draw a picture for each one and explain how information was gained or lost.

hot, dry climate	people taking objects from sites and giving them to museums	bright sunlight
Ancient Egyptian letters and records	X-rays	models and paintings
grave robbers	floods	tombs being underground

Information Gained	Information Lost
The hot, dry climate has helped to preserve objects made of wood and paper.	

Children should:
- recognise that we can learn about Ancient Egyptian life from tomb models and paintings.

Background

The purpose of the artwork in tombs was to provide for the dead person in the afterlife, when the model or picture would be transformed into the real thing. It was, therefore, more important to make sure that everything was included in a painting, than to create a realistic representation. This explains why people are always drawn with all of their limbs showing and why objects are grouped together rather than shown in their actual location. The copy of the wall painting on page 13 shows Sennedjem and his wife, harvesting the cereal crop. The model plough is made of wood and the parts are tied together with strips of leather. Simple tools could be used because the soil was so easy to work.

Wine was expensive in Ancient Egypt because the vines had to be irrigated. The illustration shows the wine makers pulling the grapes off the stalks and treading them in a large tub. The juice flowed out of a spout and was put into the wide-mouthed pottery jars to ferment. The bag press was used to extract the remaining juice from the pulp. Once most of the sugar had converted to alcohol, the wine was strained into different jars and stopped with rolled rushes and wet clay.

Fishing in Ancient Egypt was for sport as well as food; tomb paintings show people enjoying a day at the river. The simplest and earliest boats were made of papyrus reeds tied with twine, like the ones shown on page 15. There is an oarsman at each end and between the boats is a dragnet, held up in the water by floats, about to be pulled in by the crew. Traps, hooks and lines, and harpoons were also used to catch fish.

Starting Points	Main Activity	Simplified Activity	Extension Activity
E6 *'Tomb painting and model'* Remind the children about wall paintings and models in tombs; why they were there and what we can learn from them.	Look at the painting and model with the children and discuss what the people are doing and why. Read the labels and explain any unfamiliar words. Talk about the presentation of a display: the need to sequence text left to right and up to down for people to read, but also to place the text near the area it refers to. Photocopy the sheet on to thin card for a 3D display.		
E7 *'Making wine'* Explain the process of making wine in general terms. Talk about the purpose of tomb paintings and why pictures are not always realistic.	Ask the children to look carefully at the drawings and to work out what each part represents. Ask them to discuss the process in pairs before they write their instructions.	Give the children a copy of the sheet with sentence beginnings: *First collect the …* *Put the grapes into a …* Ask them to complete the sentences.	Give the children another copy of a tomb painting representing an aspect of Ancient Egyptian life. Ask them to write their own interpretation.
E8 *'A fishing trip'* Talk about the first Egyptian boats made of papyrus reeds. If possible, show a picture.	Ask the children to talk about the picture in pairs and say what is happening. Encourage them to look at details. Tell them that the story will use their observations of the model and their imagination.	Ask the children to label the picture and then, either by drawing or writing, to show what happened before the scene and what happened after it.	Ask the children to imagine being an Ancient Egyptian artist. Give them a description of how bread was made, for example, and ask them to represent it in the traditional style either by model or painting.

Plenary

Display pictures of tomb paintings and models and ask the children to prepare a talk to a group of visitors to a museum. They should explain the style and purpose of the pictures as well as the content. Ask for some volunteers to give their talk while the rest of the class pretend to be the visitors.

Tomb Painting

Tomb Model

Tomb painting and model

- Cut out the model, the painting and the labels. Use them to create a museum display. Give your display a title.

This painting is from the tomb of a man called Sennedjem.

His wife is collecting the crop in a basket.

The yoke is on the necks of the cattle and would be tied to their horns.

Ancient Egyptians grew barley, flax and wheat.

The soil from the floods was soft and easy to work.

This model shows a farmer ploughing.

He is cutting the crop with a wooden sickle.

The blade of the plough turns the soil to make it ready for planting.

Cattle are pulling the wooden plough.

Making wine

● Use the pictures and the words in the box to write the instructions for making wine in Ancient Egypt.

grapes	harvested	tub	tread	juice	spout	grape skins
	linen bag	twisted	bag press	pottery jars	ferment	

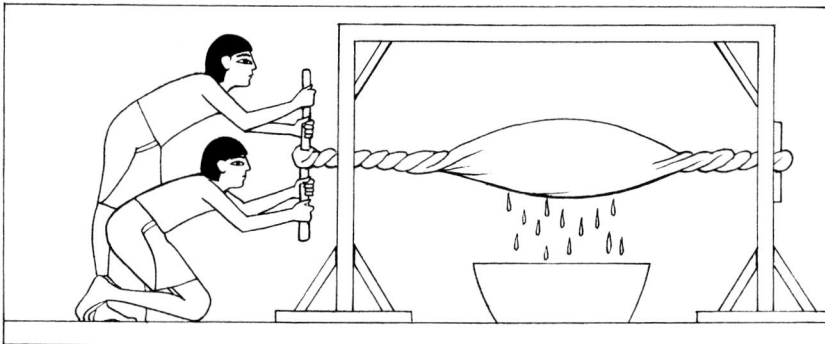

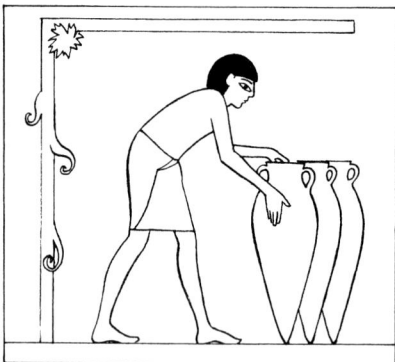

How to make wine in Ancient Egypt:

_____

_____

_____

_____

A fishing trip

Imagine you are a fisherman in Ancient Egypt.

● Use the information from the tomb model of fishermen and their boats below, and write the story of your fishing trip on the Nile.

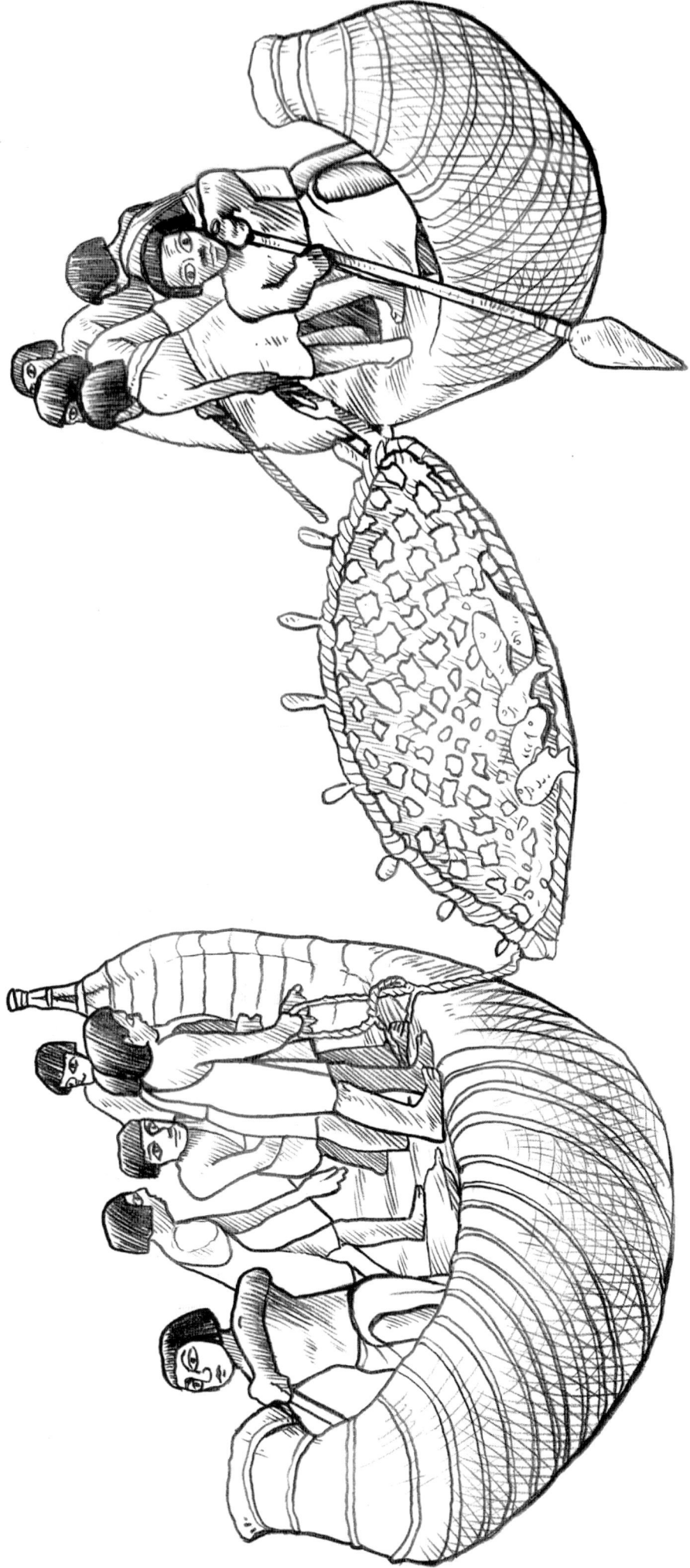

Children should:
- appreciate the value of manuscripts as a source of information about Ancient Egypt, and the significance of the Rosetta stone in understanding them.
- understand the high status of writing for the Ancient Egyptians.

Background

The Ancient Egyptians carved texts on tomb and temple walls in a script called hieroglyphs. Over time, faster forms were developed for everyday writing ('hieratic' and 'demotic' scripts). The last examples of these scripts date from the fifth century. The Egyptian language continued to be spoken and was known as Coptic and written with the letters from the Greek alphabet. This language died out and was replaced by Arabic, the language of Egypt today. Until the discovery of the Rosetta Stone and the work of Jean-François Champollion, the meaning of all Ancient Egyptian writing had been lost.

The letter of Sennefer, Mayor of Thebes, to Baki, his tenant farmer (page 18), is a rare example from the reign of Amenophis II (1427–1400BC). The letter was written on papyrus, rolled up and sealed, but Baki did not read it, as the seal was found unbroken. The translation of the word 'wiwi' is not known; no doubt children will be able to guess at a modern equivalent! Most Ancient Egyptians could not read or write. Scribes painted hieroglyphs on temple walls but the craftsmen who carved the symbols could not understand them. Scribes were usually sons (and occasionally daughters) of scribes, who then had access to positions of power in the government or army, or as priests. The scribe spent many years at school learning how to write. The wall painting on page 19 is from the tomb of a landowner called Nebamun.

Starting Points	Main Activity	Simplified Activity	Extension Activity
E9 *'The Rosetta Stone'* Explain how the written and spoken language of the Ancient Egyptians died out and that no one could read inscriptions on tombs and temples until 1822.	Tell the children that the paragraphs explain how the code to Ancient Egyptian writing was cracked, first by the discovery of a stone, then by the work of a Frenchman. Ask them to cut out the paragraphs, read them and place them in order. Tell them to check with a partner before reporting to you.	Tell the children the story of the Rosetta Stone and Jean-François Champollion. Ask them to re-tell the story in the style of a comic strip.	Ask the children to use the information to write a report of either the discovery of the stone, or the breakthrough made by Jean-François Champollion in the style of a sensationalist newspaper article.
E10 *'A letter from the mayor'* Introduce the Mayor of Thebes; show where he lived on a map and when he lived on a timeline.	Tell the children to imagine that they are the tenant farmer who works for the Mayor. Read the letter together. Find clues that the Mayor is not happy with their work, then ask them to make the list.	Make sure that the children understand the letter. Give them visual or word prompts (plants, wood, milk) and ask them to write the list.	Ask the children to record all of the deductions that can be made about this period of Ancient Egypt from the letter, for example, *They picked flowers for offerings.*
E11 *'The scribe'* Explain that most Ancient Egyptians couldn't read or write; that this was limited to a small number of privileged people.	Remind the children that the artist has not drawn the objects in a realistic position and that not everything shown was actually together at the same time.	Make sure the children complete the sheet with the help of another child who is able to read the sentences.	Ask the children to find out some other uses of writing for Ancient Egyptians. If possible, use the British Museum website. www.ancientegypt.co.uk

Plenary

Draw a large Venn diagram, label the circles 'Writing today' and 'Writing in Ancient Egypt' and ask the children to contribute to each area. Examples: *nearly everyone can write / a lot of writing was carved on walls / people sent letters.*

The Rosetta Stone

- Cut out the paragraphs, read them and stick them in the correct order.

At the age of 18, Jean-François began to study the writing on the Rosetta Stone. An important clue had already been discovered: the names of important people had loops round them. These names would be the same in all the languages. But Jean-François still thought that the rest of the hieroglyphs were just picture symbols.

In 1799 the French army was in Egypt. An engineer officer called Pierre Bouchard found a solid black stone near a place called Rosetta. It had three different types of writing: hieroglyphs, a later type of Egyptian writing, and Greek. Now scholars could use the Greek to work out how the hieroglyphics worked. But everyone thought that the symbols represented pictures and not sounds and no one could work it out.

He went on to translate all of the writing on the Rosetta Stone, and in 1828 he travelled to Egypt to see the hieroglyphs on the temples and tombs. He made notes and drawings and then spent three years writing them up. After that, aged only 41, he had a stroke and died. He had lived just long enough to achieve his childhood dream.

When he was a boy Jean-François Champollion was shown a collection of Egyptian objects with hieroglyphs. He was told that no one could understand this writing and he decided that when he grew up he would find out what it meant.

Early Ancient Egyptians used a special form of writing in symbols called hieroglyphs. The walls of the tombs and temples are covered with hieroglyphs. Later Egyptians changed to a faster way of writing and for hundreds of years no one knew what the hieroglyphs meant. But the mystery was solved by the discovery of a very important stone.

As a teenager Jean-François studied Coptic. This language was not spoken any more but it had the same routes as the old Egyptian language.

In 1822 Jean-François received some more hieroglyphic writing and he realised that all of the hieroglyphs represented sounds. Also he realised that the sounds were the same as Coptic, the language he had learned. Now he could crack the code!

A letter from the mayor

This letter is from the Mayor of Thebes in about 1420BC to Baki, the man who looked after his farm.
Hu and Cusae are towns to the north of Thebes in Egypt.

Sennefer, Mayor of Thebes

The mayor of the southern capital Sennefer speaks to the tenant farmer Baki son of Kyson to the following effect. This letter is brought to you to tell you that I am coming to see you when we moor at Hu in three days' time. Do not let me find fault with you in your duties. Do not fail to have things in perfect order. Also, pick for me many plants, lotuses and flowers, and others worth offering. Further, you are to cut 5000 boards and 200 timbers; then the boat that will bring me can carry them, since you have not cut any wood this year – understood? On no account be slack. If you are not able to cut them you should approach Woser, the mayor of Hu. Pay attention: the herdsman of Cusae and the cowherds who are under my authority, fetch them for yourself in order to cut the wood, along with the workmen who are with you. Also, you are to order the herdsmen to prepare milk in new jars in anticipation of my arrival – understood? You are not to slack, because I know that you are a wiwi, and fond of eating in bed.

- Imagine you are Baki, the man this letter was written to. Make a list of the things you have to do to prepare for the visit of your boss.

_____

_____

_____

_____

The scribe

This wall painting is from the tomb of a landowner called Nebamun.

- Read the labels and fill in the missing words below.

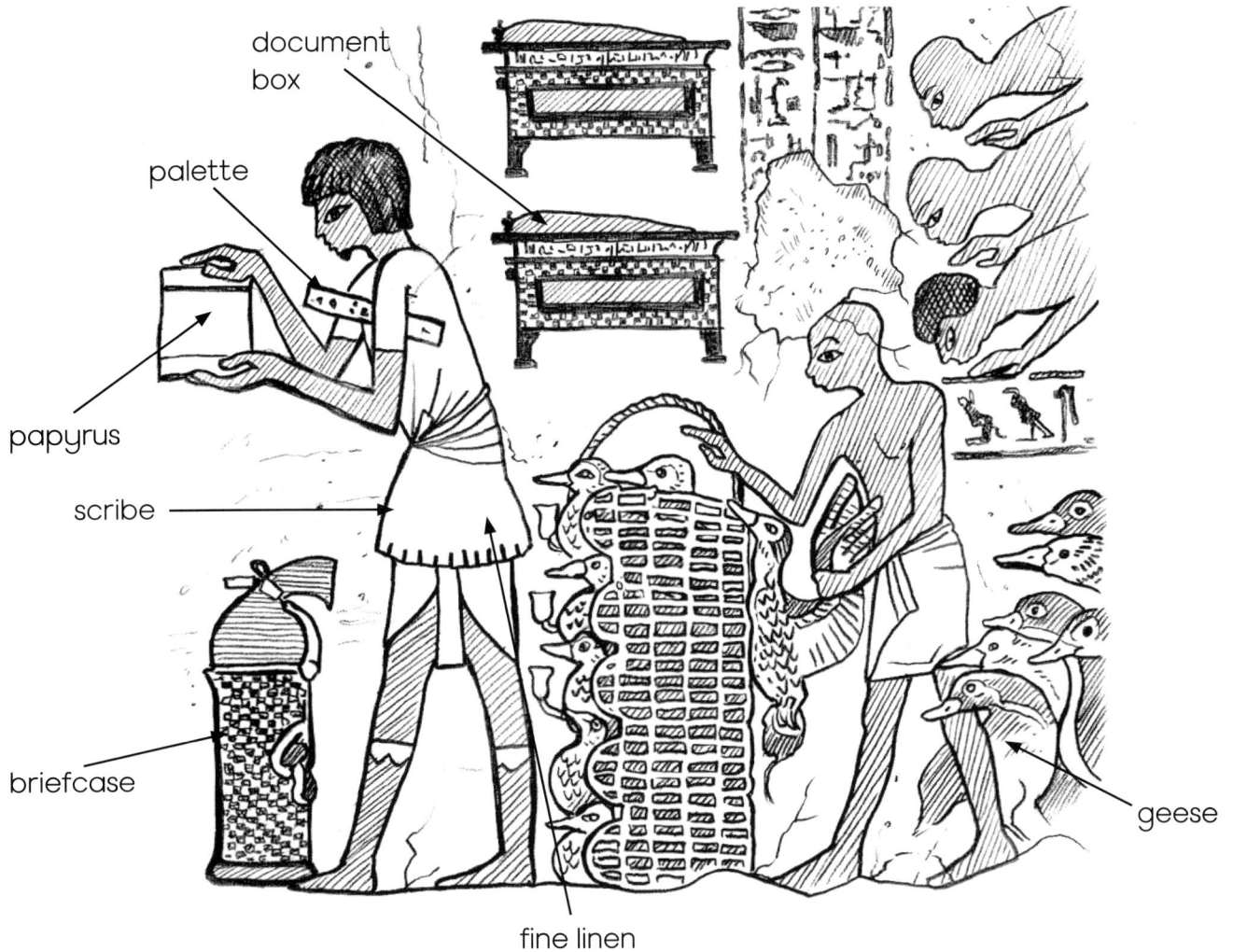

document box

palette

papyrus

scribe

briefcase

geese

fine linen

This young _____ is wearing clothes of _____ _____ because

he has an important job. He is writing on sheets made of _____ .

He stores old documents in a _____ _____ . He has a box like a

_____ to carry rolls of papyrus and extra brushes and ink. He has a

_____ made of wood or ivory to hold his brushes and ink. He is writing down how

many _____ the landowner has.

- Write a sentence about a scribe's training and possible future work.

Training	Future Work

Children should:
- understand that during the Ancient Egyptian period, technology advanced.
- know that our understanding of Ancient Egyptian building methods is not certain.

Background

The first metals that the Ancient Egyptians used were gold and copper, which they could find as lumps of pure metal. At some point they discovered that they could heat copper ore to extract the metal. The next important invention was blowpipes or bellows in about 1500BC; fires could then be made hot enough to melt and mould copper into useful shapes for tools or weapons. A later discovery was that by adding a little tin to the copper it became easier to pour, and harder than copper alone. This mixture is bronze, and the Ancient Egyptians used it in the 'lost wax casting' method described on page 21.

The shaduf is a piece of simple technology that is still used today. Without it, water would have to be carried up the bank by people or animals. No special tools, machines or pictures have ever been found to help us to understand how the Ancient Egyptians built the pyramids. Egyptologists came up with the theories that are the subject of page 23. Water in a channel will always flow to make a flat level, so builders could dig channels across the area for the base of a pyramid, and then level the ground until it was all the same distance from the top of the water. Wooden sledges have been found, giving weight to the most popular theory for raising the granite blocks that form the walls of the pyramids: they were dragged up a ramp of rubble which grew higher along with the pyramid.

Starting Points	Main Activity	Simplified Activity	Extension Activity
E12 *'Making a bronze statue'* Show a photograph of a bronze statue and explain the discovery of how to make bronze and the lost wax casting process.	Ask the children to cut out the pictures. Talk about what is happening in each picture. Ask them to read the sentences and match them to the pictures.	Give the children some pictures already labelled. Ask them to match the remaining images.	Give the children a range of resources. Ask them to research the metals used in Ancient Egypt and to write an account of how the technology changed.
E13 *'The shaduf'* Talk about the importance of irrigation in a desert climate.	Read the first paragraph with the children and discuss ways of moving water (ancient and modern). Ask them to examine the drawing in pairs and give a verbal report before they complete the written task.	Make sure that the children understand the problem and can explain how the shaduf works. Ask them to draw a second picture to show how the water gets into the irrigation channel.	Give the children the materials and tools to construct a model of the shaduf. (Flexible twigs/ wood, string, a pebble, modelling clay for the base, paper or thin card for the bucket.)
E14 *'Building the pyramids'* Look at pictures of pyramids and discuss the lack of information about how they were built.	Ask the children to work in pairs or small groups. Explain that the activity is like a puzzle and they should try to come up with a way to solve it together. Discuss the solutions as a class before asking them to write down a theory.	Make sure the children understand the problems to be solved. After discussing the problems, ask them to choose one of the problems and draw how they think the Ancient Egyptians carried out the task.	Ask the children to use what they have learned to design a page about pyramids in a book on Ancient Egypt, for younger readers.

Plenary

Summarise what the class has learned about Egyptian technology. Divide the board into three columns and make a list of processes (making a statue/wine/pyramid/ploughing); the materials involved (wood/copper/tin/granite); and the tools and equipment used (kiln, bag press, chisel, sledge, plough).

Making a bronze statue

● Cut out the instructions. Match them to the pictures.

Now cover the wax with more clay. Leave a hole in the top.

Make the shape of the statue with clay. Stick bronze pins into it.

Heat copper and tin until it is liquid. Pour the liquid into the space left by the wax.

When the liquid has cooled down, break the clay off and file away the pins. You now have a hollow bronze statue!

Cover the shape with wax and carve the fine details.

Put the model into a kiln. The heat will make the clay hard and melt the wax.

The shaduf

The problem:

The crops needed water. There was hardly any rain. Ancient Egyptian farmers had to get the water from the river. After the flood, the level of the river was lower than the fields. They needed to lift the water and pour it into their irrigation channels.

● Label this picture with the following words:

fields   irrigation-channel   bank   river

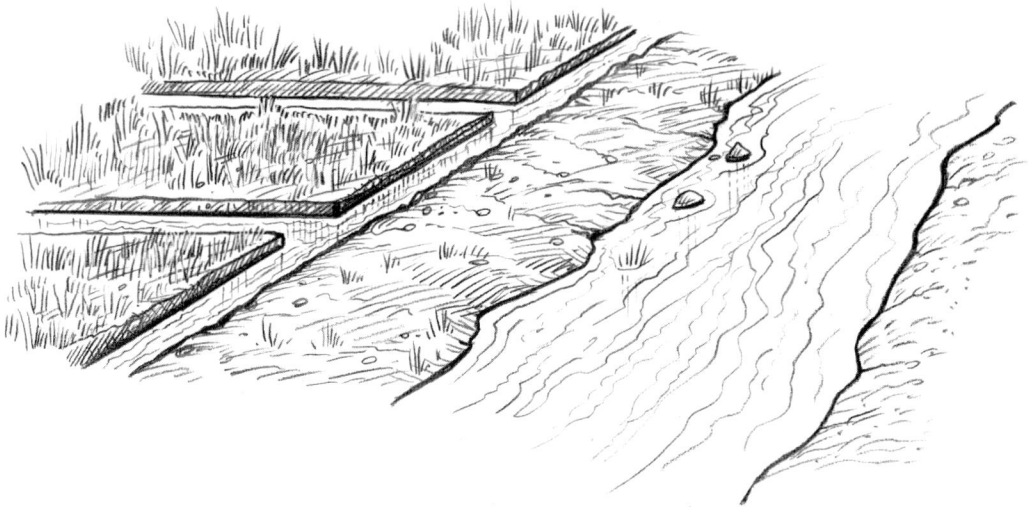

The solution:

● Explain this invention.

_____

_____

_____

_____

_____

_____

_____

● What would the farmers have done before the shaduf was invented?

_____

_____

_____

Building the pyramids

There is very little evidence about how the Ancient Egyptians built the pyramids.

● Use the pictures and clues to come up with a theory for how they did these things. Draw your solutions and write a caption underneath.

1. How did they make the ground level?

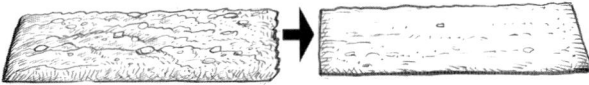

Clues:
channels   water   dig

2. How did they lift the stone blocks?

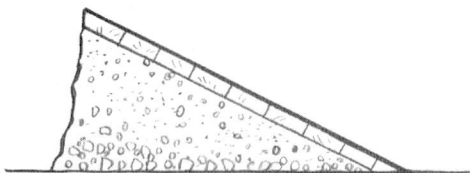

Clues:
ramp   rubble   gangs of workmen
wooden sledge

Children should:
- know where the Vikings came from.
- understand the terms 'settlement' and 'invasion' in relation to the Vikings.
- know that information about the Vikings comes from a range of sources.

Background

The Vikings were farming and seafaring people from Norway, Sweden and Denmark who raided and colonised wide areas of Europe from the ninth to the eleventh century. They did not have a common leader but shared similar culture and technology. The ethnic origin of the various raiders, traders, invaders or settlers is not always known, but it is accepted that the groups who colonised the north-west of Scotland were from Norway whereas Danish Vikings invaded England from the east. The reason for leaving their homeland in search of new territories was probably overpopulation. Britain attracted settlers because of its fertile land and resources. The plentiful supply of manpower must also have helped to assemble a raiding party.

In the past, a lot of the evidence about Vikings came from 'sagas', stories that describe Viking exploits. Although still useful, the sagas are now considered to be unreliable evidence: they weren't written down until two or three hundred years after the events they describe, they include imaginative detail and their purpose was to glorify or tell a good story rather than convey accurate information. The most reliable evidence comes from burial and settlement sites as the objects can tell us a lot about the people who made and used them. Evidence from these sources is limited however, as wood, textiles and other organic materials have decomposed. Aerial views of sites are useful, but Vikings tended to adopt the local building methods, and their settlements are in the same pattern as those of Anglo-Saxons.

Starting Points	Main Activity	Simplified Activity	Extension Activity
V1 *'Where the Vikings came from'* Place the Vikings on a timeline. Talk about how the Vikings left their homeland and how they travelled.	Give atlases to the children and ask them to work in pairs to find where the Vikings came from. Remind them that the Vikings travelled by sea, before they draw the arrows.	Give children support in finding the Scandinavian countries in an atlas. Mark the areas where the Vikings settled in Britain and ask them to read the paragraph and draw two arrows to show where these Vikings came from.	Give the children a range of resources and ask them to find the names of some of the Viking settlements in Britain.
V2 *'Raiding and settling'* Talk about the reasons that the Vikings had for leaving their homeland and for raiding other towns.	Look at the objects with the children and discuss their uses, before they draw them next to the figures. Ask them to cut out the reasons and to work in pairs to sort them.	After the children have drawn the objects, ask them to write a sentence next to each picture to say what the Viking wants (e.g. *I want more land / to get rich*).	Ask the children to imagine being a Viking settler in the north of Scotland and to list the jobs they would need to do to make their new home and farm.
V3 *'Clues about the Vikings'* Talk about the ways that archaeologists and historians find out about the Vikings and the accuracy of the sources that they use.	Ask the children to imagine that they are historians. Discuss each type of evidence in pairs or groups and report to the class before recording the accuracy of the evidence and the problems that might arise from using each source as evidence.	Ask the children to work with a partner who can help them to read the texts and discuss the evidence with them. Give them phases (*may not be true / some things rotted away*) to write into the correct box.	Ask the children to imagine being an archaeologist who has found some Viking remains and to write an account of unearthing the objects and deciding what they were.

Plenary

Ask the children to imagine they are going to make a TV programme about the Vikings. Make a list of the information to include in the introduction. Ask for a volunteer to be the presenter.

Where the Vikings came from

The Vikings came from Norway, Denmark and Sweden. Use an atlas to find these countries, then label and shade them on the map.

● Read these sentences and put arrows on your map to show where the Vikings came from.
Vikings from Norway settled in the north of Scotland and north-west England. Vikings from Denmark settled in the north and east of England. Vikings from Sweden travelled into Germany and Russia.

Raiding and settling

● Draw these objects next to the Viking who will use them.

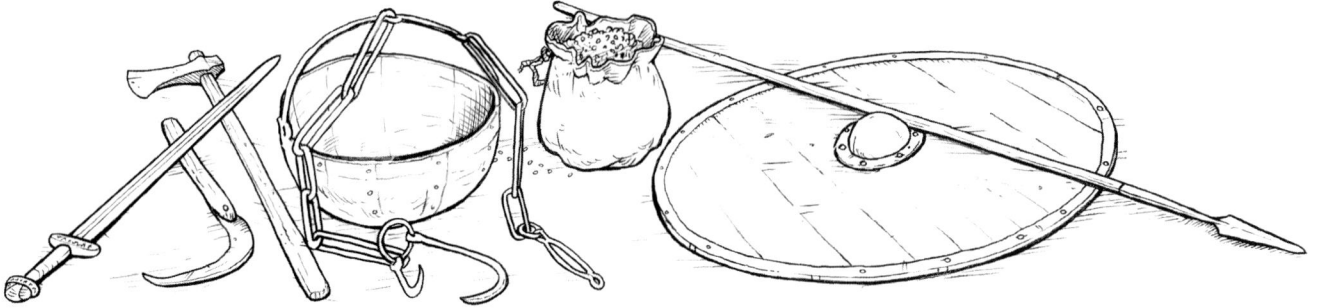

Viking settler	Viking raider

● Cut out these reasons for raiding or settling and stick them next to the correct Viking picture.

I have heard that there are monasteries on the coast with great riches.	If I get more silver and precious stones I can trade them.
Where I live, all the good land is already taken.	The soil here is good for farming.
My ship is fast; I can get away quickly.	If we stay here we can grow more food and have more animals.
Here, there are less people than where I come from.	If I have a good trip, I will get rich quickly.

Clues about the Vikings

- Discuss these types of evidence and write about the accuracy of the sources and the possible problems for each one.

Viking Objects

Objects from Viking times that have been dug up from the ground and preserved.

Viking Burials

Vikings buried rich people with all their belongings. Sometimes this included a whole ship! Some of these ships, bodies and belongings have been found and preserved.

Writings by Anglo Saxons

Terrible warnings appeared in Northumbria. There were great flashes of lightning. Fiery dragons were seen in the air. That same year the enemies of God horribly destroyed God's church in Lindisfarne.

Viking Settlements

Bird's eye view of a place where Vikings lived.

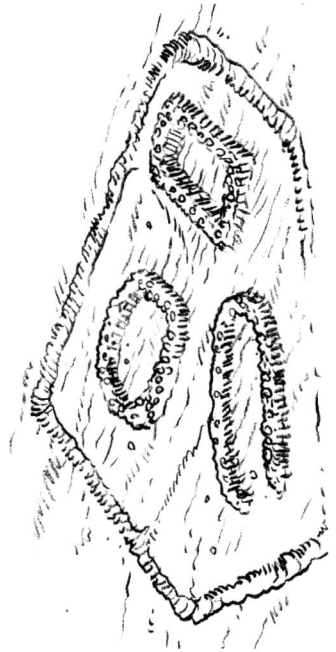

Viking Sagas

Stories about the Vikings that were written down two or three hundred years after the Vikings lived.

Children should:
- learn how found objects tell us about Viking activities and buildings.
- know that place names can tell us where the Vikings settled.

Background

York has a long-term urban history as both a Roman and Anglo-Saxon settlement. It had been an important royal, ecclesiastical and trading centre for 450 years when, in 865, the Vikings reached Northumbria. The Anglo-Saxon Northumbrians were engaged in civil war and it was comparatively easy for the Vikings, led by Ivarr the Boneless, to overrun the city in 866. Control of York was continually disputed and the last Viking leader, Eric Bloodaxe, was driven out in 954. The Vikings are well known for raiding and pillaging. The excavations in York have shown them also to be civic organisers, planners, architects, road makers, artisans, artists and traders. The wet ground below the city helped to preserve objects which tell us about the way of life of the Vikings who lived there. These objects have been used in a recreation of Viking life in the Jorvik Viking Centre in York, England.

The consistent size of houses in York suggests that people built to regulations. A rectangular timber frame was built over an earthen floor. Triangular sections held up the roof rafters, which were covered in thatch (bundles of reeds). The walls were made of wattle (woven hazel twigs) and daub (clay and straw). Remains were found of clay hearths in the centre of the floor, lined with stone. These would have provided light as well as heat, as there were no windows. The places where Vikings settled often retain a name that can be linked to Scandinavian languages. Knowing the meaning of the words tells us something about the origins of the place. Grimsby, for example, was the town of Grim; Boothby was a village with huts; Monksthorpe was once a village owned by monks.

Starting Points	Main Activity	Simplified Activity	Extension Activity
V4 *'The Viking settlement at Jorvik'* Tell the children about the settlement at Jorvik (York).	Ask the children to work in pairs to name the objects and materials before writing on the sheet. Discuss each object and supply vocabulary (turn clay, cast metal, spin thread, weave cloth).	Ask the children to name the objects and materials. Give them phrases or sentences to match to the objects and write them under the heading, 'What it tells us about Viking life'.	Ask the children to draw illustrations of some of the Viking activities.
V5 *'Remains of Viking houses'* Tell the children about the remains of houses found in Jorvic.	Show an example of a cutaway drawing. Talk about the materials and how the house would be constructed before asking children to produce a drawing.	Give the children a copy of the sheet with the timber frame drawn in. Ask them to complete the drawing.	Ask the children to imagine being inside a Viking house and to write a description.
V6 *'Viking place names'* Explain how a place name can tell us about its history if we know what the word means. Give some examples of Viking place names.	The day before the lesson, if possible, ask children to bring a road atlas to school. Show them how to use the atlas and ask them to work in pairs to carry out the activity.	Give the children a photocopy of an Ordnance Survey map of an area with Viking place names. Ask them to highlight the names and then record them on the sheet.	Ask the children to write an interpretation of some of the names they have found.

Plenary

Continue the idea of preparing a TV programme (see page 24). Ask the children to suggest questions and answers for the first interview of the programme, with an archaeologist from York. Then ask for volunteers to role-play the interview.

The Viking settlement at Jorvik

These objects were found under the ground.

- Name the object and the material it is made from using the words below.
- Write down all the activities the Vikings must have done to make, use or obtain these objects.

bone	leather	fish bone	clay	cloth	bowl
wool	~~lamp~~	metal	wood	shoe	coins

Object	Name	Made of	What it tells us about Viking life
			They skinned animals, cured leather and stitched leather.
	lamp		

Remains of Viking houses

- Use the evidence to finish a cutaway drawing of a Viking house.

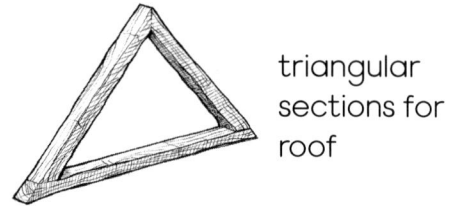

timber beams

thatch

triangular sections for roof

woven hazel twigs covered with sticky clay and straw (called wattle and daub)

- House floor measured 16m x 5m.
- Walls only high enough for one storey.
- No holes for windows found.
- Ashes from a fire in the centre of the room.

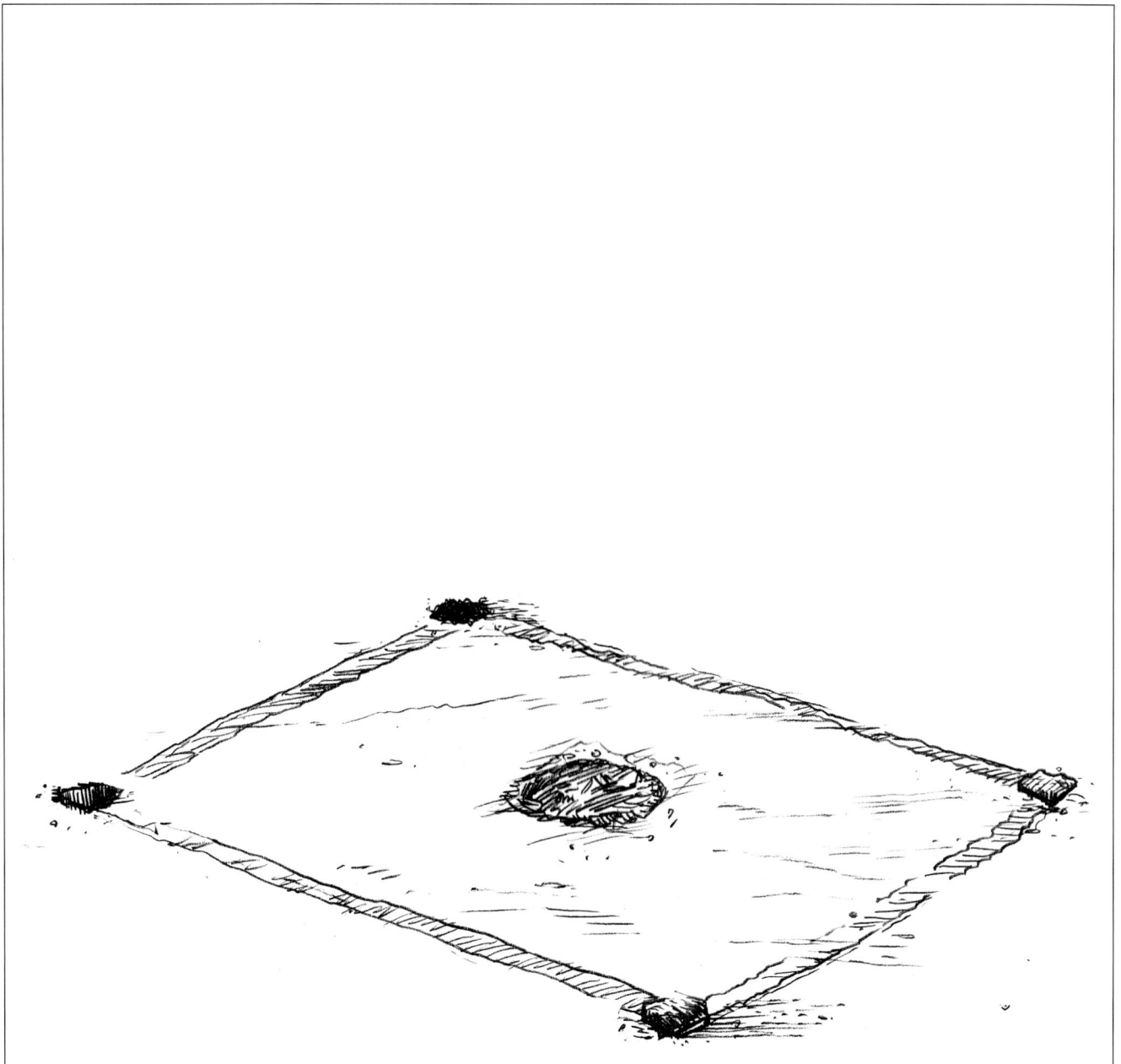

FOLENS HISTORY IN ACTION 4 © Folens (copiable page)

Viking place names

These words came from the Danish and Norwegian languages spoken by the Vikings who settled in Britain.

---

beck – a stream
booth – hut
borg – castle, fortified town
by – village
dale – valley
fell – mountain
garth – farm
gil – narrow valley

holm – island
ness – headland
tarn – small lake
thorpe – outlying farm (This might be a
    second settlement, built by
    the son of the first settler.)
thwaite – a clearing
wick – harbour or bay

● Use a road atlas index to find examples of place names with Viking words. Check which part of Britain they are in and mark them on the map. The shaded areas show where the Vikings settled.

Grimsby

Children should:

- learn how Vikings could combine farming and raiding.
- learn about the Lindisfarne Monastery as an example of a Viking raid.
- know that Viking sagas contain exciting, exaggerated stories of raids.

Background

Many Viking chieftans divided their time between farming and raiding. The raids had to be fitted between the busy times of sowing and reaping on the farm. The winter was to be avoided because of the higher frequency of storms at sea. Svein Asleifarson, a Viking sailor, lived on the island of Gairsay in Orkney in the twelfth century and his lifestyle was recorded in a saga (see page 33). The saga was written in the twelfth century and so the claims about Svein's drinking hall or the number of men, for example, cannot be taken as totally accurate.

Lindisfarne, an island just off the coast of Northumberland, was one of Britain's most sacred sites in the ninth century. In 793 Vikings approached, however the accounts were written by outraged Anglo-Saxons and the savagery of the raid might be exaggerated. The monks apparently went down to the beach to welcome the sailors, but were hacked to death or dragged into the sea and drowned. The treasure of the monastery was taken and the building was burned. While sagas may exaggerate the exploits of their heroes, they build a consistent picture of clans or groups with leaders who could assemble the necessary number of men for a raiding party. The extract on page 35 is from *Egil's Saga*, c.1230, and tells the story of an attack on Courland (modern Lithuania) from the raiders' perspective. The full version can be found in *The Complete Sagas of Icelanders*, trans. Bernard Scudder, vol. 1 (Reykjavik: Leifur Eiriksson, 1997), 71–74. Or at http://college.hmco.com/history/west/mosaic/chapter5/.

Starting Points	Main Activity	Simplified Activity	Extension Activity
V7 *'Raiding and farming'* Talk about the best times of the year for sailing, sowing and reaping in Viking times.	Read the text with the children. Relate the times of year in the text to the months in the diagram before asking them to complete it, using the pictures.	Provide the children with a copy of the sheet giving the times of the year when Svein changed his activity, and ask them to complete the diagram.	Ask the children to imagine either a good year or a bad year for Svein, and write his account of it.
V8 *'The raid of Lindisfarne monastery'* Show the children where Lindisfarne is on a map and tell them about the raid.	Discuss some ideas for a sensationalist headline and report with the children, before asking them to write the story and add a picture.	Give the children sentence beginnings for the report *(Viking ships arrived at … Monks went to meet …)*. Ask them to finish the sentences to make the report.	Give the children a range of resources and ask them to find out the sort of treasure that would have been in the monastery and report to the class.
V9 *'Egil's saga'* Talk about Viking sagas, when they were written and what their purpose was.	Read the text with the children. Discuss ways in which the story might continue. Tell them it should show how brave and clever Egil was.	Children who can only write a short ending to the story can be asked to reread the first paragraph and draw a picture to illustrate it.	Give the children a copy of the original saga to read and ask them to mark those places where the story is probably not true.

Plenary

Ask a group of children to prepare to be Viking raiders, and the rest of the class to prepare some questions, then role-play an interview with the raiders.

Raiding and farming

This was how Svein used to live. Winter he would spend at home on Gairsay in the Orkney Islands, where he entertained some eighty men at his own expense. His drinking hall was so big, there was nothing in Orkney to compare with it. In the spring he had more than enough to occupy him, with a great deal of seed to sow which he saw to carefully himself. Then when that job was done, he would go off plundering in the Hebrides and in Ireland on what he called his 'spring-trip', then back home just after mid-summer, where he stayed till the cornfields had been reaped and the grain was safely in. After that he would go off raiding again, and never came back till the first month of winter was ended. This he used to call his 'autumn-trip'.

(Taken from 'Orkneyinga Saga' from *The Complete Sagas of Icelanders*, trans. Bernard Scudder)

● Write on the diagram to show what Svein did in each season of the year. Use the pictures and the text above to help you.

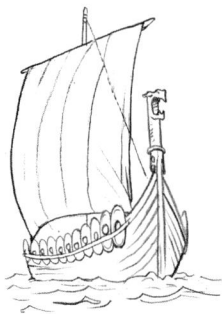

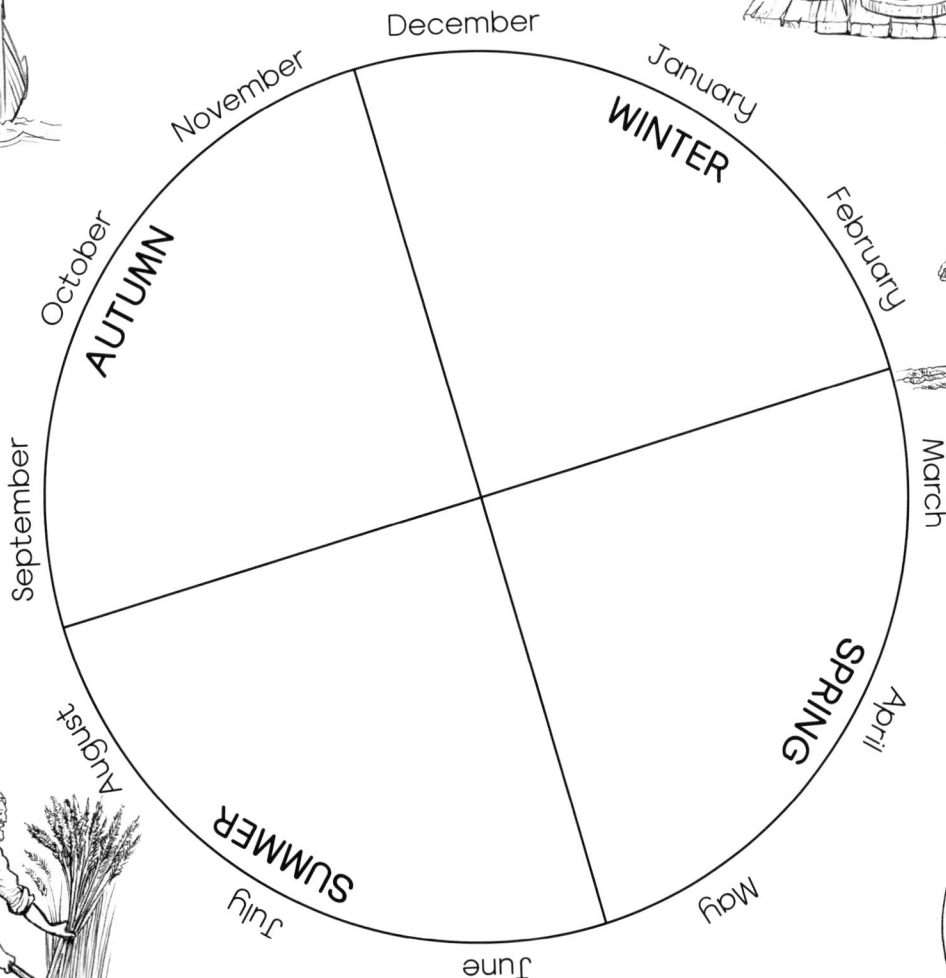

The raid of Lindisfarne monastery

- Use these words to write a report on the raid of Lindisfarne monastery in the style of a newspaper report today.

longships   round shields   swords   killed   drowned

bows   arrows   axes   spears   monks   stolen   treasure   burned

ANGLO-SAXON NEWS

8th June 793

!

    FOLENS HISTORY IN ACTION 4   © Folens (copiable page)

Egil's saga

One day they put in to an estuary with a large forest on the upland about it. They went ashore there and split into parties of twelve men. They walked through the woodland and it was not far until the first settlement began, fairly sparse at first. The Vikings began plundering and killing people at once, and everyone fled from them. The settlements were separated by woods. Meeting no resistance, the raiders split up into smaller bands. Towards the end of the day, Thorolf had the horn sounded to call the men back, and they returned to the woods from wherever they were, since the only way to check whether they were all there was to go to the ships. When they took the count, Egil and his party had not returned. By then night was falling and they did not think there was any point in looking for him.

Egil had crossed a wood with twelve men and found great plains which were settled in many places. A large farm stood nearby them, not far from the wood, and they headed for it. When they reached it they ran inside, but found nobody there. They seized all the valuables they could take with them, but there were so many buildings to search that it took them a fairly long time. When they came out again and headed away from the farm, a large band of men had gathered between them and the wood, and was advancing upon them.

(Taken from 'Egil's Saga' from *The Complete Sagas of Icelanders*, trans. Bernard Scudder)

● Write an ending to the story.

_____

_____

_____

_____

_____

Children should:
- recognise the skilled design and build of Viking ships.
- be able to imagine what it would be like to sail on a Viking ship.

Background

Well-preserved examples of Viking ships have been found in burial mounds and at the bottom of lakes. The Oseberg ship was discovered in Norway in 1903, buried beneath airtight layers of clay and peat. Viking ships were 15–30 metres long. The keel was made of one piece. A big oak block with a hole for the mast was rested on top. The boards were made from oak and sometimes pine. The ship was built so that the board plates partly covered each other and were joined together by iron nails. The joins between the planks were sealed with tar and wool. In one of the boards on top there were holes for the oars. No sails have been found but they were probably made of wool, with a web of leather strips to hold the shape. The carved dragonheads were put in place as the ship approached land.

Longships (or warships) and merchant ships were each designed to suit their purpose. Longships, were narrow and light so they were faster. They were flat-bottomed and could sail right up to shore and then be pulled on to the beach for a fast attack. There was space for oarsmen all the way down each side. Merchant ships were sturdier with a wider and deeper hull to carry passengers, animals or goods for trading. The central deeper area for cargo meant less space for oarsmen and so less speed without wind. Vikings did not have compasses. They would have been able to use the position of the sun and stars to navigate. Local knowledge of seabirds and sea creatures could help them judge the distance from shore. They could use the sail as a large tent over the whole boat, but they also had tents to sleep under on the beach and sleeping bags made of animal skins.

Starting Points	Main Activity	Simplified Activity	Extension Activity
V10 *'The design of Viking ships'* Talk about how sailing ships work and why Viking ships had oars as well as sails.	Ask the children to work in pairs and to treat the activity as a puzzle, completing all the parts they can and then spending longer on the more difficult parts. When they have finished, check the answers as a class.	Ask the children to match only a few of the design features.	Give the children information about the Oseberg ship and ask them to write an explanation of how it was preserved and reconstructed.
V11 *'Two types of Viking ship'* Explain that the Vikings changed the shape, size and materials of a ship according to its purpose.	Look at the drawing of the merchant ship together and ask the children to describe it. Make sure they understand the different purpose of a longship and that they will need to read the paragraph carefully before starting to draw.	Read the paragraph with the children and talk about the difference in the designs before asking them to draw the longship.	Give the children a range of resources to search for more information about longships. Ask them to write a paragraph about their findings.
V12 *'A journey by Viking ship'* Talk, in simple terms, about how sailors today find their way at sea. Contrast this with navigation in Viking times.	Read the sentences with the children and discuss as a class what a journey would be like. Make sure children understand that they should write in the first person.	Give the children a list of questions about their journey (*What is your name? Where are you going? What for?*) Ask them to write the answers to the questions.	Ask the children to summarise what they have learned by producing a page on ships in a book about Vikings for younger children.

Plenary

Continue the making of a TV programme about the Vikings (see pages 24 and 28). The next interview is with an expert on Viking ships. Ask the children for questions then let them rehearse in pairs as interviewer and expert before choosing some children to perform their interview for the class.

The design of Viking ships

iron nails

sail

leather strips

tarred wool

removable carving

wooden chest

rudder

keel

oar holes

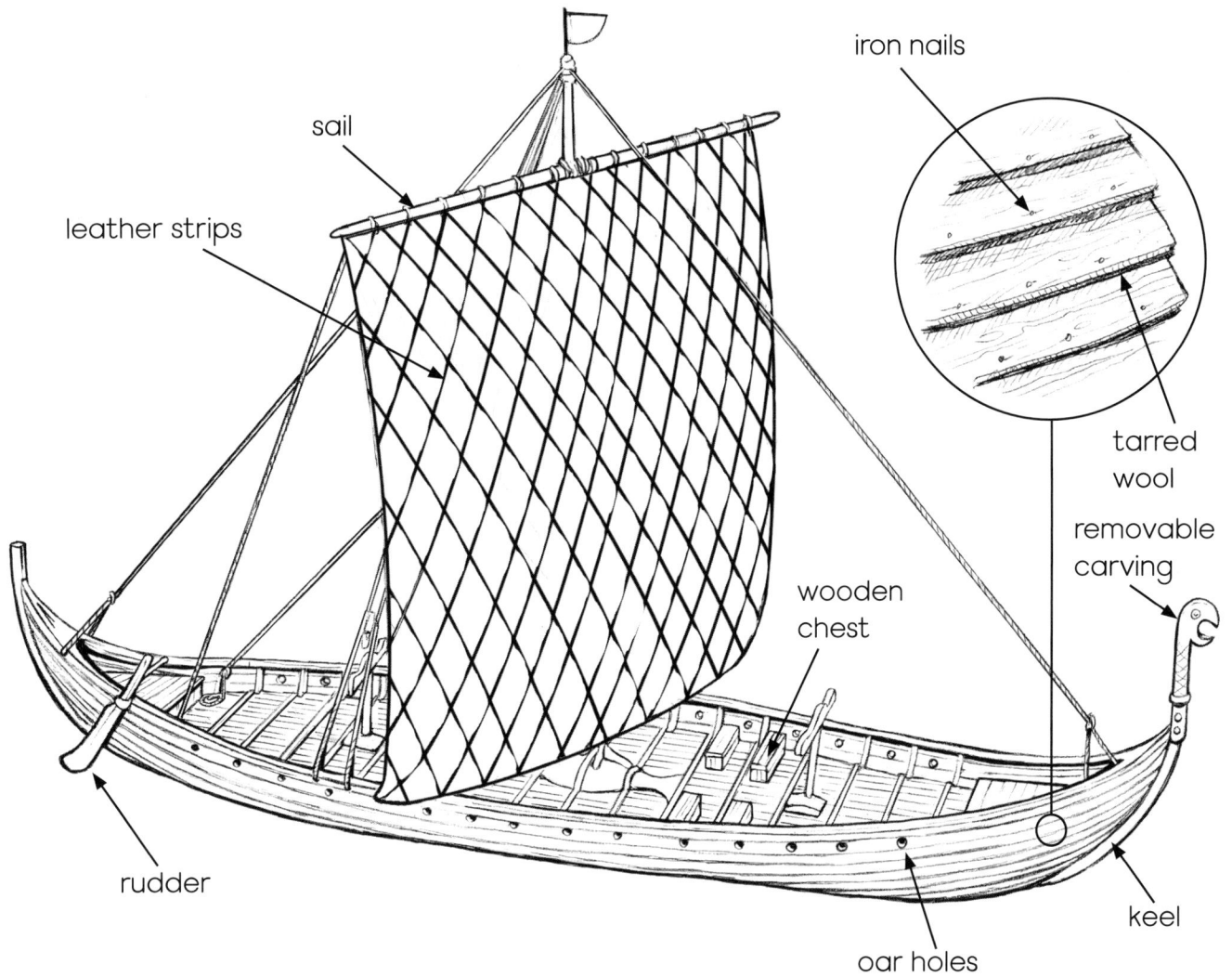

● Match each design feature to its purpose.

to help the sail keep its shape	leather strips
to make the ship waterproof	
to make rowing easier	
to sit on and store belongings	
to make the ship go in a straight line	
to steer the ship	
to catch the wind	
to hold the planks together	
to stop it falling into the sea in rough weather	

Two types of Viking ship

● Look at the drawing of a Viking
   merchant ship.

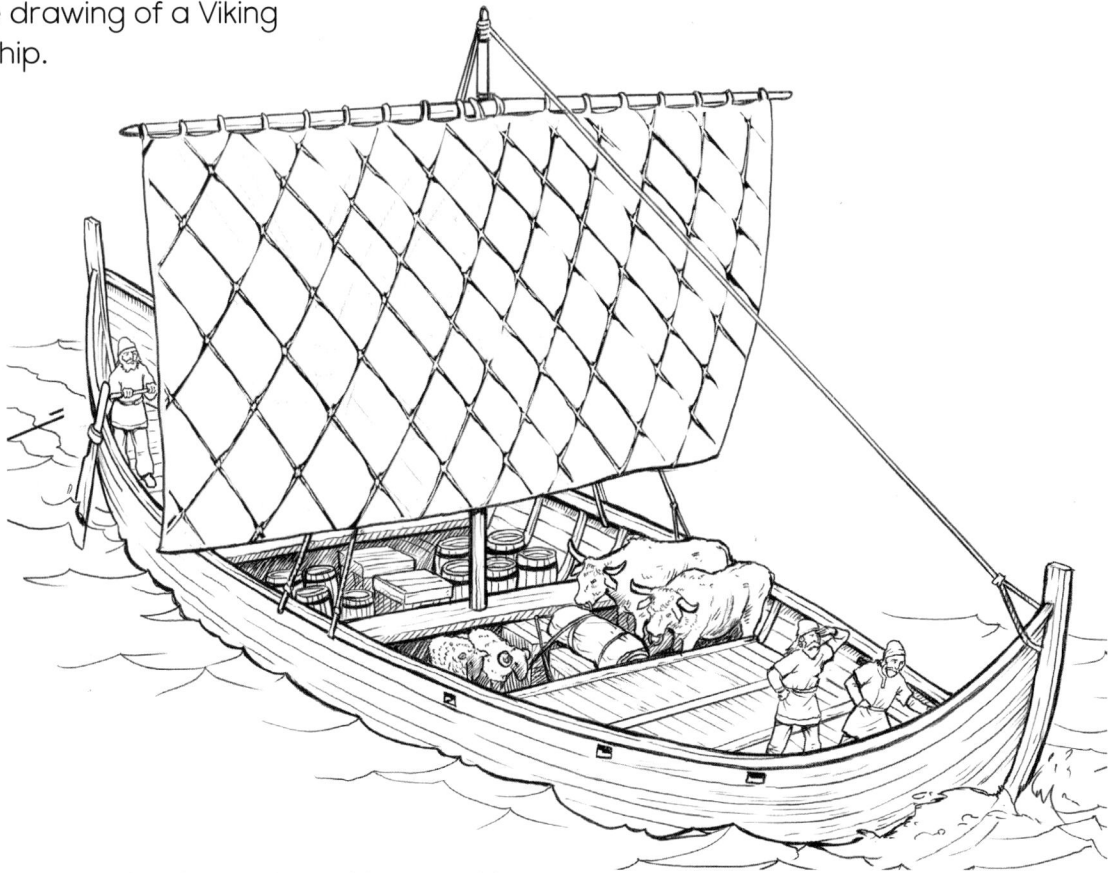

● Use this information to draw a longship (warship).

Longships were narrower than merchant ships and not as deep. They were light enough to be carried. They were fast; rowers sat all the way down each side so the boat could still move quickly without wind. There was no space for cargo and no covered area on deck. The oarsmen sat on chests; the length of each oar depended on its position on the ship.

A journey by Viking ship

● Imagine you are a Viking. Use this information to write an account of your journey.

- They always sailed within sight of land if possible.
- They used landmarks to know where they were.
- These were some of the methods they could use to navigate:
  - knowing the position of the sun and stars
  - knowing where sea animals and seabirds were normally found.
- There was no shelter on deck.
- At night they could pull their ships up on the shore.
- They could take the sail down and sleep under it like a tent.
- They could sleep under tents on the shore.
- They had two-man sleeping bags made of animal skins.
- There would be only dried food to eat, or what they could find.
- They would have to find or carry fresh water.

_____

_____

_____

_____

_____

_____

_____

_____

_____

_____

_____

- know that Vikings traded with other people.
- know that the Vikings were successful explorers in search of new land.
- know when the Vikings lived and settled in Britain.

Background

Viking traders travelled around the coast of Europe. By sailing south along the lakes and rivers of Germany and Russia they were able to meet up with traders from Arab and Far Eastern countries where they could buy luxuries such as silk, silver and spices. To sell, the Vikings took natural products such as walrus ivory, whalebone, and the furs and skins of animals. They also carried amber, a fossilised resin that was cut and polished to make beads, pendants and brooches. In the early part of the Viking period, coins were unknown. Even when they were introduced as a result of trading with eastern countries, the Vikings continued their method of weighing silver or other precious metals to use as currency.

Vikings from Norway discovered and colonised Iceland and Greenland; evidence of their settlements has been found there. Two sagas tell the story of the discovery of 'Wineland' or 'Vinland' by ships blown off course; one attributes the first sighting to Bjarni Herjolfsson and the other has Leif Eriksson being blown off course. We don't know which is correct but it seems that the Vikings were the first Europeans to land in America.

In Britain, Vikings from Norway settled in independent groups in the Orkneys and Shetland Islands from 800. The invasion and colonisation of the north and east of England after 850 by the Danes was more organised; and a truce was made with the Anglo-Saxon Alfred the Great in 886. By 954 the land had been reconquered by Anglo-Saxon kings, though England was part of the empire of Viking King, Canute, from 1013–42. England had peacefully returned to Anglo-Saxon rule when the Normans invaded in 1066.

Starting Points	Main Activity	Simplified Activity	Extension Activity
V13 *'Viking traders'* Show on a map how Vikings could travel south on rivers to trade with Arab and Eastern countries.	Set up a market place environment in the classroom. Read the text on page 41 with the children and talk about the various items to trade and their uses. Discuss what traders could ask or say about goods. Explain how Vikings used silver and provide the children with scales and something to serve as silver (modelling clay for example, which they can shape into coins or arm rings). Decide how much each item is worth. The children can have one to six cards each, depending on how long you want the activity to take. The simplest role play would be for each child to sell and buy one item. The Vikings can move from stall to stall but the market stall holders must stay in one place. Encourage the children to barter for goods.		
V14 *'Viking explorers: Leif Eriksson'* Look at a map again and explain the Viking discoveries of and settlements on Iceland and Greenland.	Ask the children to read the text carefully, to underline the places, and to talk in pairs about the places Leif went to before they draw on the map. Then go through the activity with the class.	Read the text, referring to the map. Help the children to mark the journeys on the map.	Ask the children to write an imaginative account of one part of the journey from Leif's point of view.
V15 *'A timeline of the Vikings in Britain'* Read the text together on the activity sheet.	Look at the map and the Anglo-Saxon kingdoms together. Make sure that the children understand the timeline before asking them to complete the activity.	Give the children a copy of the sheet with the significant years marked on. Ask them to read the text and write the events on the timeline.	Ask the children to make a quiz about the Vikings in Britain by writing questions on one side of the cards and answers on the back.

Plenary

Write on the board the headings: invaders, raiders, settlers, explorers, traders, farmers. Ask the children to recall what they have learned about the Vikings under each heading.

Viking traders

Vikings from Sweden travelled by river into Russia and to Eastern countries. They took goods to sell. They returned with goods from the Eastern countries. Traders used silver as money and carried scales to weigh it with.

● Some of you are Viking traders. These are the goods you have to sell or exchange.

walrus ivory	whalebone	animal furs and skins
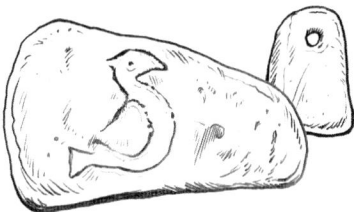		
amber	honey	wax

● Some of you are traders from Eastern countries. These are the goods you have to sell or exchange.

wine	salt	glass

silk	silver jewellery	spices

FOLENS HISTORY IN ACTION 4

Viking explorers: Leif Eriksson

● Read this text and underline all the places that Leif went to.

Leif Eriksson was born in Iceland in about 970 or 80. When he was a child he moved to a new settlement on Greenland with his parents, and grew up on their farm. As a young man he set off on a trip to Norway. His ship was blown to the Hebrides, north Scotland, and he spent the summer there. In the autumn he arrived in Norway. The King of Norway had become a Christian; Leif met him and was also converted to the new religion. The King sent Leif back to Greenland to convert people there. On the way, the wind blew the ship off course and Leif came to a land he had never seen before. He saw wheat and grapevines growing naturally. We now know that he had reached Newfoundland in the north of Canada. Leif's name for it was 'Wineland'. Leif returned to Greenland and told people about Christianity, and about the new land he had found. Soon an expedition was organised to go and explore Wineland and a group of Vikings lived there for three years.

● On the map, draw arrows to show Leif's journeys.

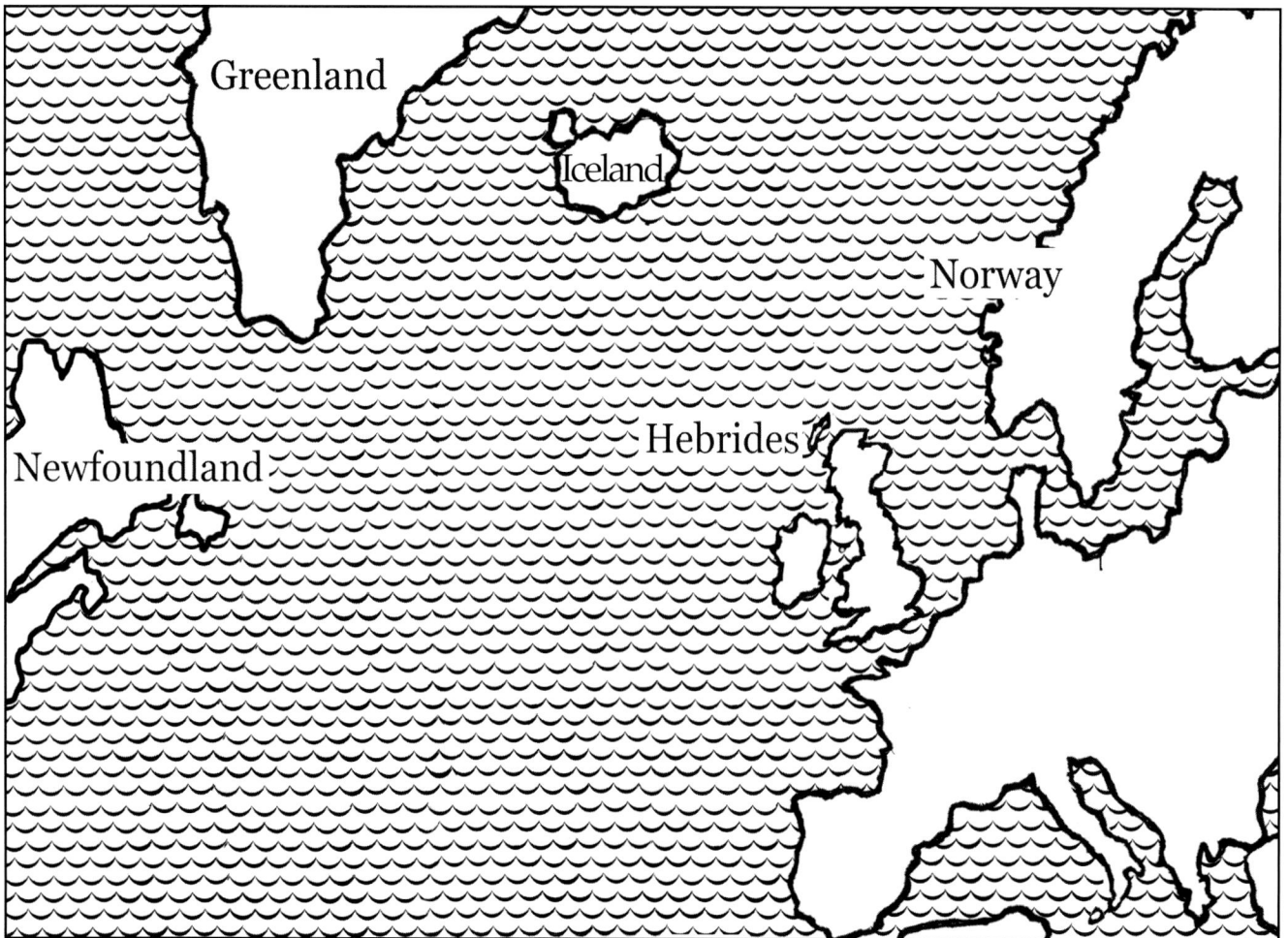

FOLENS HISTORY IN ACTION 4

A timeline of the Vikings in Britain

Saxon Britain 600–900 AD

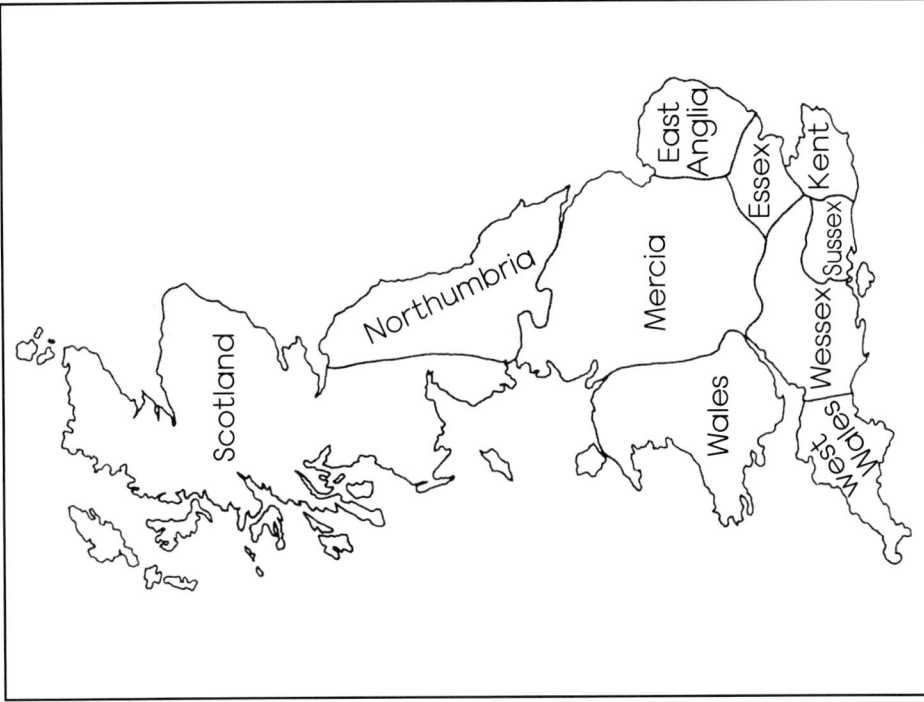

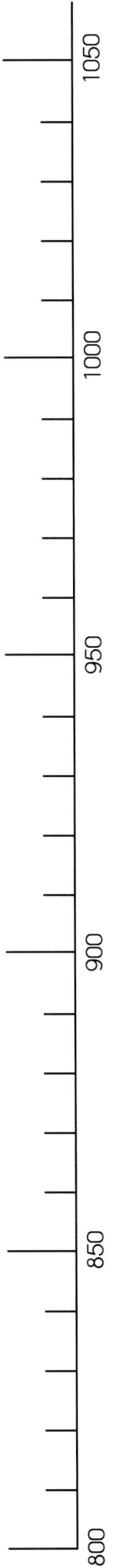

Vikings began to settle in Scotland from 800. The Danish Vikings who wanted to live in England had to fight the Anglo-Saxons. The Viking armies conquered East Anglia, part of Mercia, and Northumbria by 865. In 886 they signed a treaty with the Anglo-Saxon King Alfred. By 924 the Anglo-Saxons had re-conquered East Anglia and Mercia and by 954 they had re-conquered Northumbria as well. The Vikings started raiding England again in 980. From 1013 to 1042 England was part of the empire of the Norwegian King. England then returned to Anglo-Saxon rule until the Normans invaded in 1066.

- Write the main events on the timeline.

●

| 800 | 850 | 900 | 950 | 1000 | 1050 |

Children should:
- learn about Henry VIII: his place in the Tudor family and his character.
- learn about the role of a monarch in the 1500s.

Background

Henry VIII (1491–1547) was the second son of Henry VII, the first Tudor king. Henry's older brother, Arthur, died in 1502, just four months after marrying Catherine of Aragon. Henry VII died in 1509 and Henry VIII succeeded him at the age of 17. Shortly afterwards he married his brother's widow. Their only daughter, Princess Mary, was born in 1516. His two other surviving legitimate children were Elizabeth (daughter of Anne Boleyn) and Edward (son of Jane Seymour). Henry was both athletic and intellectual in his pursuits. He hunted every day, was a fine archer and excelled in jousting tournaments. He also read widely, wrote books on theology, played the lute and composed love songs and church music. He attended mass five times a day. In the evenings he attended court dances and stayed up late gambling at cards and dice.

Henry VIII was six feet, four inches tall, had broad shoulders, fair skin, red hair and a thin high-pitched voice. He had a huge appetite for food and drink and in later life he became very overweight. He did not take an active part in the day-to-day running of the country, leaving the work to his counsellors. He did, however, make all of the important decisions himself. He usually spent an hour or two in the evenings with his secretaries, before or after supper, dealing with correspondence. He fiercely suppressed his opponents and there were far more imprisonments and executions than in his father's day.

Starting Points	Main Activity	Simplified Activity	Extension Activity
H1 *'Henry's family tree'* Show the children a picture of Henry VIII and when he lived on a timeline. Explain that this is called the Tudor period, after the surname of his family.	Demonstrate how to draw a family tree, using the children's own families as examples. Tell children to read the information on page 45 to complete Henry VIII's family tree. Make available a range of resources and ask them to find and draw portraits of the kings and queens and add the dates.	Give children a copy of the activity with only information about Henry VIII's parents and siblings. Ask them to complete the first two lines of the tree only.	Give the children a range of resources and ask them to find out the names of the mothers of each of the children of Henry VIII in the family tree.
H2 *'A description of Henry'* Explain some of the ways in which we know about Henry VIII, and that because it was so long ago some facts are more certain than others.	Make sure that the children understand the meanings of the headings under which they are going to group the cards. Tell them to work in pairs and to discuss each card before placing it in a group.	Reduce the number of cards for the children to sort. If necessary, also reduce the number of headings.	Ask the children to write about Henry VIII in the style of a lonely hearts' column. *Young monarch seeks suitable queen. He is … She must be …* etc.
H3 *'Henry VIII's power as king'* Talk about the way that countries are governed and how monarchs in Europe had a lot more power in the past.	Make sure that children understand all of the vocabulary before asking them to illustrate the things that Henry could do.	Ask the children to complete only the first activity.	Ask the children to use the information they have learned so far to write an imaginary 'Day in the life of Henry VIII'.

Plenary

Write the following words on the board: portraits, his library books, his suits of armour, letters from people at his court. Ask the children to consider what these things tell us about Henry VIII. How reliable is this evidence?

Henry's family tree

● Use the information below to draw Henry VIII's family tree.

■ Henry VIII was the second son of Henry VII, who was the first Tudor king.
■ Henry VII was married to Elizabeth of York. She had four children. The first was a son, called Arthur. Arthur died, so the second son, Henry, became the next king
■ Henry VIII's older sister was called Margaret; his younger sister was called Mary.
■ Henry had many children but only three of them lived long enough to become king or queen. They were Mary I (1516–58), Elizabeth I (1533–1603) and Edward VI (1537–53).

The Tudor Kings and Queens

m

b. 1457 d.1509

b. 1466 d.1502

b. 1491 d.1547

b.   d.

b.   d.

b.   d.

A description of Henry

● Cut out the cards below and sort them under the following headings:

Appearance   Personality   Physical Ability   Intellectual Ability

Good at jousting	A fine archer	Six feet, four inches tall	Red hair and fair skin
Composed music	Read lots of books	Enjoyed hunting	Liked to eat and drink a lot
Wrote books about religion	Had broad shoulders	Got fat in old age	Spoke French and Latin fluently
Played the lute	Charming to pretty women	Liked gambling and dancing	Wore expensive clothes

Henry VIII's power as king

Here are some of the things that Henry VIII could do as king.

- Draw pictures to illustrate.

Declare war on another country.	Discuss politics with foreign visitors.	 Dictate letters to his secretary.
Decide to raise more taxes.	Make a new law.	Give one of his castles to someone he liked.
 Have somebody executed.	Lead his army into battle.	Spend money on buildings.

- Write about what a monarch can do today.

_____

_____

_____

_____

Children should:
- understand the main reasons and events leading to the marriage of Catherine of Aragon.
- know why Henry wanted to divorce Catherine.
- understand the consequences of the divorce.

Background

Catherine of Aragon was the daughter of Ferdinand and Isabella of Spain. At three years of age she was betrothed to Arthur, eldest son of King Henry VII of England. For her parents, the marriage meant that England would be an ally against France. For Henry VII, as well as making an ally of Spain, he would get a large dowry with Catherine. Catherine sailed to England at the age of 15 and married Arthur, but he died a few months later. She then spent seven miserable years in dismal castles with no money while Henry VII tried to get the rest of the dowry. He betrothed his second son to her but later changed his mind. We do not know for sure why Henry VIII decided to honour the original agreement and marry her once he was king in 1509, but they were seen to be very happy together for the first years of their marriage, which lasted for 23 years.

Only when it became obvious that he was not going to have a son did Henry VIII start to look for a way out of the marriage. In 1527 Henry asked Pope Clement VII for an annulment. The Pope would not come to a decision because he did not want to anger either Henry or the Holy Roman Emperor Charles V, who was Catherine's nephew. The problem became known as 'The King's Great Matter'. Henry waited for six years but when Anne Boleyn became pregnant, possibly with a son, he could wait no longer and declared himself Head of the Church of England. His archbishop, Thomas Cranmer, then issued the decree of nullity, and Henry married Anne Boleyn in 1533. Henry closed the monasteries on the grounds that they were immoral, but seized their land and possessions which gave him a lot of wealth, some of which was spent fighting wars.

Starting Points	Main Activity	Simplified Activity	Extension Activity
H4 *'Catherine of Aragon'* Talk about the way that royal marriages were used to make alliances between countries.	Look at the picture of Catherine, and explain the words 'dowry' and 'betrothed' to the children. Ask them to read the sentences in pairs and work out the order.	Give the children a copy of the sheet with most of the sentences in order, and ask them to correctly place the remaining three or four.	Ask the children to write about the reasons for the actions of the King and Queen of Spain, Henry VII and Henry VIII.
H5 *'The King's great matter'* Talk about the attitude to children in the 1500s, and why Henry wanted a son so much.	Talk about the dilemma for Henry and for the Pope. Explain the term 'annulment' before asking children to complete the sheet. Tell the children what Henry decided to do and ask them to write it in their own words.	Give children the pictures of the Pope, Henry and Catherine with one empty thought bubble each. Ask them to write one thought for each person.	Ask the children to add a drawing and a thought bubble for Anne Boleyn.
H6 *'The consequences of the divorce'* Talk about the short- and long-term consequences of the divorce.	Make sure that children understand how the diagram works by drawing a similar diagram of something familiar to them. Ask the children to work in pairs to complete the boxes.	Give the children a copy of the sheet with only one consequence to be entered for each of the four sentences on the left-hand side.	Give the children a range of resources and ask them to find out what happened to Catherine after she was sent away from court. Ask them to report their findings to the class.

Plenary

Ask the class to imagine they are writing a book about Catherine of Aragon. What would be the heading for each chapter? Ask them to list some of the key events that would go in each chapter.

Catherine of Aragon

Catherine of Aragon

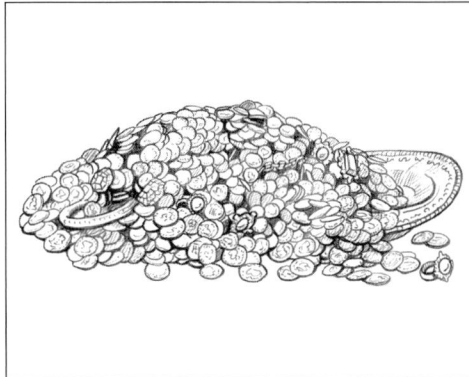

dowry

betrothed

● Cut out the sentences and stick them in the right order.

Henry VIII married Catherine.

After Henry VII died, Henry VIII became King of England.

When she was three years old she was betrothed to Prince Arthur of England.

Henry VII betrothed Catherine to his second son, Henry.

Catherine and Arthur were married.

Catherine of Aragon was the daughter of the King and Queen of Spain.

At age 16 she travelled to England, bringing with her a large dowry.

Four months after the wedding, Arthur died.

Catherine had to stay in England without any money, and wait.

Catherine and Henry were crowned King and Queen of England.

The King's great matter

- Cut out the people and the thoughts and match them together.

If I marry Anne Boleyn I might have a son.

I am Henry's true wife. I will never agree to a divorce.

Catherine is too old to have any more children.

Perhaps God is punishing me because I married my brother's widow.

If I annul Henry VIII's marriage, Charles V will be angry.

If I don't annul the marriage, Henry VIII will be angry.

Henry VIII

Pope Clement VII

Catherine of Aragon

- Write about what Henry did to solve his problem.

The consequences of the divorce

- Copy the sentences into the correct box.

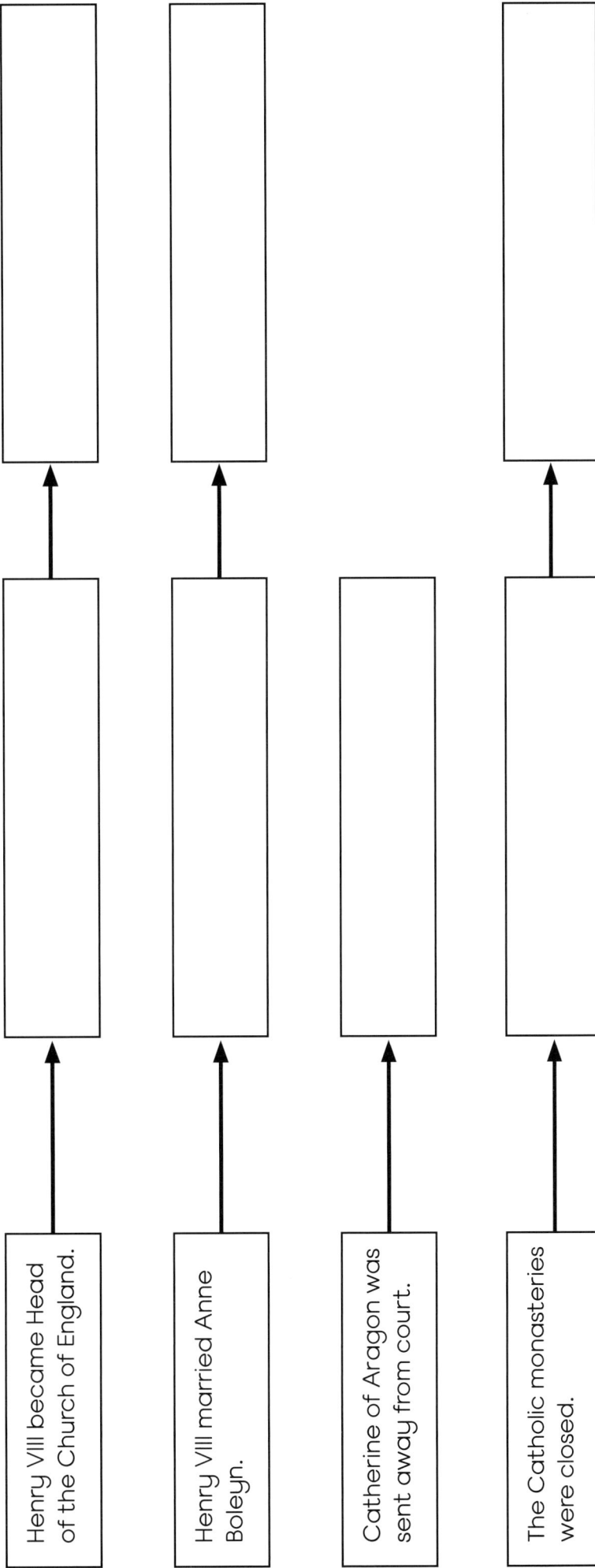

Cause	Consequence
Henry VIII became Head of the Church of England.	
Henry VIII married Anne Boleyn.	
Catherine of Aragon was sent away from court.	
The Catholic monasteries were closed.	

When she was older, Elizabeth became queen.

Henry got a lot of money.

England eventually became a Protestant country.

Catherine did not see her daughter Mary again.

Anne's daughter, Elizabeth was born.

The Protestants became more powerful.

He used some of the money to fight wars.

- learn that rivalry was a significant feature of life at the royal Tudor court.
- know why Henry had Anne executed and why he married Jane.

Background

Anne Boleyn's place and date of birth are uncertain: possibly at Blickling in Norfolk in 1500/1501. At the age of 12 or 13 she was sent to the court of Louis XII in France to wait on Queen Mary, Henry VIII's sister. She learned fluent French and enjoyed French poetry and music. In 1522, a year after returning to England, she is recorded as attending the court. She was a lady-in-waiting to Queen Catherine when Henry fell in love with her. Unlike her sister Mary, she did not give in to his advances until she seemed very likely to become the next Queen. Her pregnancy pushed Henry into breaking with Rome in 1533 and marrying her. There was some disappointment when the child was a girl (Elizabeth). After two miscarriages and with Henry's growing interest in Jane Seymour, Anne's enemies plotted against her and charges of adultery and incest were brought. In 1536 she was tried in the Great Hall of the Tower of London. She denied all the charges in a dignified manner, but was found guilty and executed.

Jane Seymour was born in 1509. Her family home was in Wiltshire and it may have been on a visit there in 1535 that Henry noticed her. She was already a lady-in-waiting to Anne Boleyn and may have also attended Queen Catherine. The first evidence of Henry's interest in her is in early 1536. She is reported as having a calm and gentle manner but there are different opinions as to her true feelings and thoughts. Henry and Jane were married soon after the execution of Anne Boleyn. During her pregnancy in 1537 Henry tenderly indulged her every whim. Jane gave birth to a son, Edward. She lived long enough to attend his christening but died two weeks after the birth.

Starting Points	Main Activity	Simplified Activity	Extension Activity
H7 *'Life at court'* Explain the word 'court' as the people who surrounded the King (advisors, attendants, visitors) and who participated in dances and other entertainments.	Read the text about life at court with the children and make sure that they understand any new vocabulary. Look at examples of magazine articles before asking them to complete the task.	Make sure that the children have understood the key points about life at court. Encourage them to illustrate these points and write a few sentences for each picture.	Ask the children to research and write about what happened to people at King Henry's court if they would not do what he wanted.
H8 *'Marriage to Anne Boleyn'* Tell the children about the courtship and marriage of Henry and Anne. Look at a portrait of Anne.	Make sure that the children understand where Anne is at the time of the letter and why.	Give the children a copy of the sheet with the letter partially written and ask them to fill in the missing words and phrases.	Give the children copies of portraits of Anne and ask them to write a description of her appearance.
H9 *'Marriage to Jane Seymour'* Look at a portrait of Jane. Recall Henry's interest in her as one of the factors in the execution of Anne. Explain the difference between fact and interpretation.	Ask the children to work in pairs to divde the sentences into 'fact' or 'possible'. The 'facts' can then be ordered chronologically. Establish that the diary might include facts but will be an interpretation.	Ask the children to do either the sorting activity or the diary extract.	Give the children a range of resources and ask them to find more facts and interpretations for Jane Seymour.

Plenary

Draw a timeline of Henry's life from birth (1491) to the death of Jane Seymour (1537) and ask the children to contribute as many events as they can.

Life at court

The King was always surrounded by his advisors, by people in important jobs and men and women from wealthy and important families. These people were called the court. At court different groups and families competed to get the King's attention and be the favourites. If the King liked them, then there would be favours: a position of power, money, some land, even a castle or palace. There was plotting and scheming; people would spread rumours against their enemies.

At the court of King Henry VIII these groups or families often used a pretty woman to get the attention of the King and favours for their group. If a woman was one of the attendants to the Queen, she was in a good place to catch the King's eye. Noble women were taught poetry, to sing and dance. They would be expected to make witty conversation.

● Imagine that you visited the court of King Henry VIII for a day. Write a report about life at the court in the style of a modern article. Include drawings to illustrate the article.

Marriage to Anne Boleyn

- Imagine you are Anne Boleyn in the Tower of London.

  Use the words in the box to write about your situation, in the style of a letter to a modern magazine problem page.

husband	loved me	daughter
wanted a son	tired of me	afraid
executed	loves another woman	

FOLENS HISTORY IN ACTION 4   © Folens (copiable page)

Marriage to Jane Seymour

● Write the word 'fact' or 'possible' next to each of these sentences.

She was born in 1509.	
She was a 'lady-in waiting' for Anne Boleyn.	
Henry VIII fell in love with her.	
She deliberately tried to get Henry's attention.	
Henry and Jane were married in 1536, after the execution of Anne Boleyn.	
She seemed calm, but was really afraid.	
She seemed calm because she didn't understand the situation.	
She died in 1537, two weeks after her son was born.	
She had one son, called Edward.	
She is the only one of Henry's wives to be buried with him.	

● Choose one of the important days in Jane Seymour's life.
   Write an extract from her diary for that day.

Date:

_____

_____

_____

_____

_____

_____

Children should:

- know why Henry married Anne of Cleves and why he divorced her.
- know why Henry married Catherine Howard and why he had her executed.
- know that Catherine Parr was his last wife and that she outlived him.

Background

After the death of Jane Seymour, Henry remained single for over two years. His next marriage was politically motivated. He looked for an ally among the other countries that had separated from Rome. The Duke of Cleves, a duchy on the Rhine, was Protestant and had two daughters. In 1539, Hans Holbein was sent to paint them; Henry chose Anne (1515–57) and the marriage was arranged. When Henry saw Anne in person he was disappointed; he said she looked like a horse. The marriage went ahead in January 1540 but he immediately wanted to end it. Anne very sensibly co-operated and they were divorced by July. She was to be known as 'the King's sister' and she was given residences including Hever Castle. She apparently lived quite happily in England and was a visitor to the court.

When he married Anne, Henry was already interested in Catherine Howard (born c.1521) and he married her 16 days after the divorce. She was 19 years old, vivacious and pretty and he was very much in love with her. Henry did not believe the first reports of her adultery but agreed to an investigation and was persuaded by the evidence. In February 1542 she was executed, like her first cousin Anne Boleyn. Catherine Parr (born 1512) was a very different sort of woman; she had already been widowed twice and was known to be intelligent, caring and sensitive. She and Henry were married in July 1543. Henry was now suffering with an ulcerated leg; she nursed him and helped to soothe his temper. She also looked after the interests and education of his children. Envious of her influence, a faction at court plotted against her, but she found out and rushed to tell the King that her enemies had told lies and that she was his loyal wife. Henry died in 1547 and Catherine married Thomas Seymour but died after giving birth to a daughter in 1548.

Starting Points	Main Activity	Simplified Activity	Extension Activity
H10 *'Marriage to Anne of Cleves'* Look at a copy of the Holbein portrait of Anne and tell the children about the marriage.	Read the text and look at the pictures with the children. Ask for suggestions for the missing text and pictures before they complete the activity.	Give the children a copy of the sheet with more of the story added and ask them to complete the remaining text or pictures.	Ask the children to write sentences about how the story could have ended differently. If Holbein's portrait had made Anne look ugly … and so on.
H11 *'Marriage to Catherine Howard and Catherine Parr'* Look at portraits of Catherine Howard and Catherine Parr and tell the children about their marriages to Henry.	Ask the children to read the words and phrases in pairs and agree where the information should go before completing the table.	Give the children a copy of the table with some of the information already filled in and ask them to complete it with the remaining words and phrases.	Give the children a range of resources and ask them to find out more information about each of the wives.
H12 *'The six wives game'* Recall each of the six wives, what happened to them and which had children who survived. Practise the phase: 'Divorced, beheaded, died, divorced, beheaded, survived.'	Photocopy the activity sheet on to thin card. Read the instructions with the children and make sure everyone understands the rules. The game could be played in pairs, or groups of three or four. It will probably work best if children with mixed reading ability are grouped together. Point out to the children that there are different ways to make a pair: 'first wife' could pair with 'Catherine of Aragon' or 'divorced'. (Although pairing with 'divorced' would leave two 'Catherine of Aragon' cards, so you could decide to disallow pairs without a name!)		

Plenary

Write the words 'why, what, when, where, who' on the board and ask the children to work in teams to produce questions about Henry and his wives. They must know the answers themselves. Use the questions to hold a quiz.

Marriage to Anne of Cleves

- Complete the story of Henry and Anne of Cleves.

	3. Anne came to England.	4. Henry did not like the look of Anne!
1. Henry VIII sent Hans Holbein to paint the daughters of the Duke of Cleves.	2.	
5.	6. Anne agreed to a divorce.	7.
		8. Anne lived happily in England until she died. She sometimes visited the court.

Marriage to Catherine Howard and Catherine Parr

• Copy the information below into the correct box in the table.

a widow known for her caring, sensitive personality

1512

accused of being unfaithful and executed

Parr

an attractive, lively 19-year-old girl

Catherine

about 1521

Catherine

Howard

1543

the death of Henry VIII in 1547

1540

Biographical information	Fifth wife	Sixth wife
First name		
Surname		
Born		
Description		
Date married to Henry VIII		
Reason for end of marriage		

The six wives game

● Cut out the cards, shuffle them and spread them out on the table, face down. Take it in turns to turn over two cards. If they refer to the same person, keep them. If not, turn them over again. The winner is the person who has collected the most cards at the end of the game.

first wife	second wife	third wife
fourth wife	fifth wife	sixth wife
Catherine of Aragon	Catherine of Aragon	Anne Boleyn
Anne Boleyn	Jane Seymour	Jane Seymour
Anne of Cleves	Anne of Cleves	Catherine Howard
Catherine Howard	Catherine Parr	Catherine Parr
divorced	beheaded	died
divorced	beheaded	survived
Elizabeth Tudor	daughter of Anne Boleyn	Mary Tudor
daughter of Catherine of Aragon	Edward Tudor	son of Jane Seymour

Children should:

- know when World War Two took place and which countries were involved.
- know who the British and German leaders were and their role in the war.
- be able to sequence the events leading up to the war.

Background

Adolf Hitler became Chancellor (prime minister) of Germany in 1933. Laws against Jews, communists and trade unionists were passed. Support for his policies was fuelled by the humiliating peace terms inflicted on Germany at the end of World War One and the poor state of the German economy in the following years. In August 1934 he was overall leader (Führer) of Germany with dictatorial powers. The size of the army was expanded. Hitler's expansionist plans were known about and local authorities in Britain were advised to prepare for an air attack as early as 1935. In 1938 Germany took over Austria and Czechoslovakia. When Poland was invaded in 1939 the British Government said that unless Germany withdrew, Britain would declare war on Germany.

British Prime Minister, Neville Chamberlain, announced the war on 3 September 1939. Britain was allied with France. Italy and Japan fought with Germany and the three are referred to as the Axis powers. The Soviet Union and the United States later joined the Allies. Chamberlain had tried to avoid war with Germany until the invasion of Poland in 1939. He was an uninspiring wartime leader and was forced to resign in May 1940. Winston Churchill, a strong leader and gifted orator who had always opposed Chamberlain's policy of appeasement, replaced him in May 1940 and led the wartime coalition government until the elections after the end of the war in 1945.

Starting Points	Main Activity	Simplified Activity	Extension Activity
W1 *'World map 1939'* Talk about how WW2 began and list the countries that fought.	Explain the terms 'Axis' and 'Allies'. Provide the children with atlases and ask them to identify the numbered countries.	Give the children a copy of the map with a few of the countries already identified.	Give the children a suitable book or text and ask them to find and shade those countries that were invaded by Germany during the war.
W2 *'Leaders of Britain and Germany in World War Two'* Show the children photographs of the three leaders. Explain the role played by each leading up to the beginning of the war.	Ask the children to work in pairs to read the sentences and match them to a leader. Tell them that there are three statements for each person.	Take the key words and phrases from the statements and give them to the children with the drawings of the leaders. Ask them to match the words and drawings.	Give the children a range of resources; ask them to find out more about one of the leaders and report their findings to the class.
W3 *'Timeline for the beginning of World War Two'* Explain how the terms of the end of World War One were very hard on Germany and how this contributed to another war.	Ask the children to read the events in pairs and to discuss the order. Point out that two events can occur in the same year. Check the results as a class before asking them to write the events on the timeline.	Give children a reduced number of key events to sequence.	Ask the children to write a news report announcing the start of the war.

Plenary

Work with the class to construct a paragraph that will introduce the topic of World War Two for a museum display.

World map 1939

- Use an atlas to label the countries on the map.

③

⑦

⑥

⑤

②

①

④

Key

Allied Countries

① _____

② _____

③ _____

④ _____

Axis Powers

⑤ _____

⑥ _____

⑦ _____

Leaders of Britain and Germany in World War Two

Adolf Hitler

Neville Chamberlain

Winston Churchill

● Cut out the statements and pictures and match them to the correct leader.

He was the Prime Minister from May 1940 until the end of the war.

He thought it was best to let Hitler take over some countries.

He blamed Jews and Communists for the problems in Germany.

He lost the support of the other politicians and he resigned in May 1940.

He was a dictator; he could change the laws himself.

He thought that Britain should stand up to Hitler.

He tried to avoid going to war with Germany.

He was a strong leader; he inspired people to support the war effort.

He was good at public speaking; he could get the support of a crowd.

FOLENS HISTORY IN ACTION 4 © Folens (copiable page)

Timeline for the beginning of World War Two

- Write the events on the correct place on the timeline.

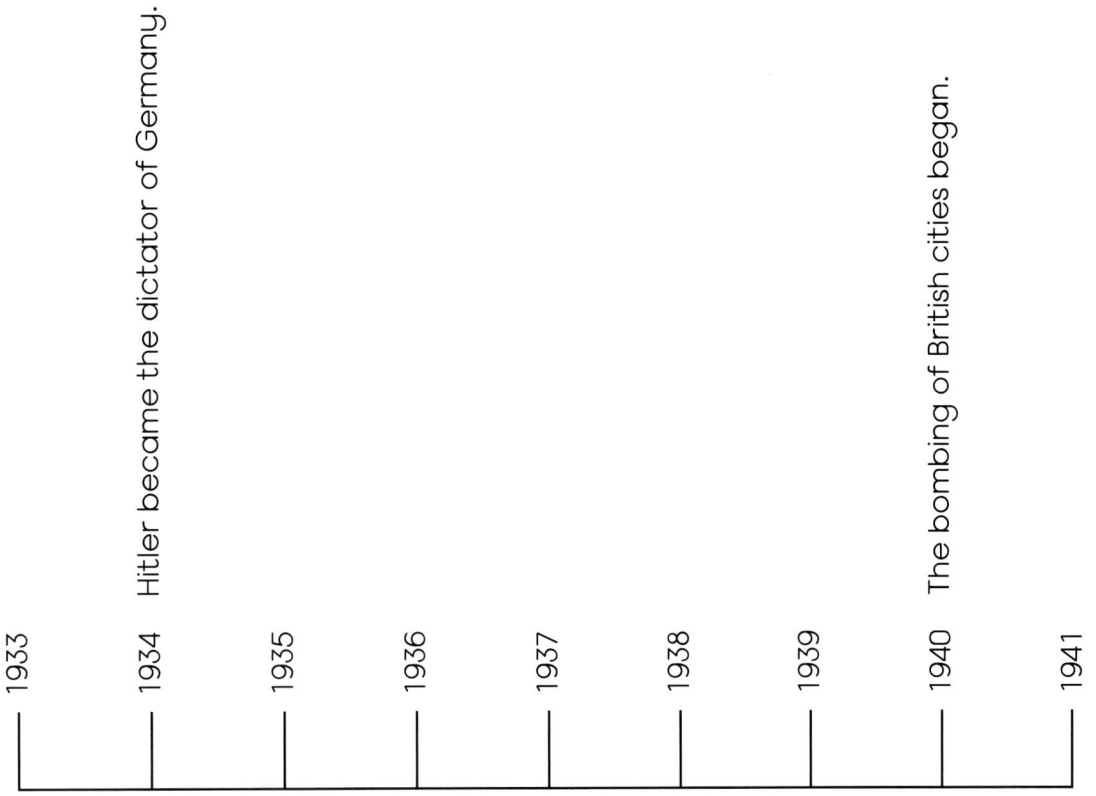

1933

1934   Hitler became the dictator of Germany.

1935

1936

1937

1938

1939

1940   The bombing of British cities began.

1941

- Adolf Hitler, leader of the Nazi Party, became Prime Minister of Germany.

- Hitler made laws against Jews.

- Hitler became the dictator of Germany.

- Hitler made the German army bigger.

- The British Government started to make plans for an air attack from Germany.

- Germany took over Austria and Czechoslovakia.

- The German army invaded Poland.

- Britain and France declared war on Germany.

- Chamberlain resigned and Churchill became prime minister.

- The bombing of British cities began.

Children should:
- learn about internment as an example of the climate of fear created by war.
- learn about some of the ways in which the war affected home life.

Background

At the beginning of the war the government was very worried about 'enemy aliens' – Germans, Austrians or Italians, living in Britain. It was thought that they might give valuable information to the Germans. Posters reminded people not to talk carelessly where they could be overheard. There were 75 000 Germans and Austrians in Great Britain in 1939. Many of them, like Renate's family (see page 65), were escaping persecution by Hitler.

When war began, preparations had already been made for the evacuation of children from cities that might be bombed to the countryside. This was organised through schools and over one million children were evacuated in 1939, but many returned by January 1940 when the expected air raids did not take place. They were evacuated again at the start of the Blitz in September 1940. Evacuees were 'billeted' with adults, who received extra rations to feed them.

The government had prepared for chemical warfare by issuing everyone with gas masks. Children practised wearing their gas masks in school and once the war had started they had to carry them at all times in a box, strapped round their necks. The blackout was put into operation on 1 September 1939. In order to make towns and cities invisible to enemy aircraft no lights were to show at night. Street lamps were extinguished and blackout curtains hid any light from houses. Every street had a warden who would go round and check the blackout and could issue fines to people who had not complied. In spite of safety measures thousands of people died in accidents in the dark. Navigation in an unfamiliar area was also difficult as signposts were removed to make it harder for any spies to find their way around.

Starting Points	Main Activity	Simplified Activity	Extension Activity
W4 *'Internees'* Talk about the fear of invasion during the war, the people who would be suspected of spying and the sort of idle talk to be avoided.	Read the text about Renate with the children. Discuss the reasons for her arrest. Ask the children to make a general list of reasons for arresting people at the time.	Make sure the children have understood the story. Ask them to list the three reasons why Renate was arrested.	Ask the children to write a letter from Renate to her mother, telling her what has happened.
W5 *'Evacuation'* Talk about the evacuation programme. Read an extract from a suitable fictional account, such as *Carrie's War* by Nina Bawden (published by Puffin).	Ask the children to read the text in pairs and to discuss together what is happening. Ask them to imagine they are explaining to some one who knows nothing about the war.	Ask the children to work with a partner who will read the text to them, and to discuss the text with the same partner. Give them some of the words they will need to write a brief explanation.	Ask the children to think up questions to ask somebody who was evacuated during the war. They could then swap their questions with a partner and try to answer them.
W6 *'Protecting Britain from the enemy'* Show photographs of gas masks, removed sign posts, and blackout curtains and explain the safety measures, reasons and consequences.	Make sure that children understand how the table works before asking them to complete it.	Give children a copy of the sheet with some of the boxes filled in and ask them to complete the rest.	Remind the children about the job of the air-raid warden. After they have completed the main activity ask the children to write an extract from the warden's dairy.

Plenary

Collect together photographs or replicas, and children's work for pages 65–67. Arrange them for a museum display and ask the children to prepare an explanation for a guided tour of the museum. Ask for some volunteers to deliver their talk.

Internees

Renate Scholem was a German girl who escaped to England with her mother after her father had been sent to a concentration camp. Read about what happened to her at the start of the war.

Renate was at boarding school in Ramsgate. On 27 May 1940 the police arrived and told her to pack a suitcase. She was not allowed to phone her mother. She was being arrested because she had read some books that were not approved of. She was living near the coast and they thought she might help invading Germans. Also, she had been seen talking to a man in RAF uniform; perhaps she was getting information from him. (This man was really her brother-in-law, but no one believed her.)

Still wearing her school uniform, Renate was taken to Holloway prison. The next morning she had to queue up with the other women to empty her slop bucket. They were all internees. One was a German nun who had been in a convent in England for twenty years. Another was an English woman who was married to a German and had been visiting her family when the war broke out.

Renate was sent to the Isle of Man, along with thousands of people with German or Italian connections. While the camps were being organised, conditions were bad and some prisoners fell ill. The hardest thing for internees was being separated from their families and friends and having no news.

● Give reasons why a person could be 'interned' during the war.

_____

_____

_____

_____

_____

● Explain this poster.

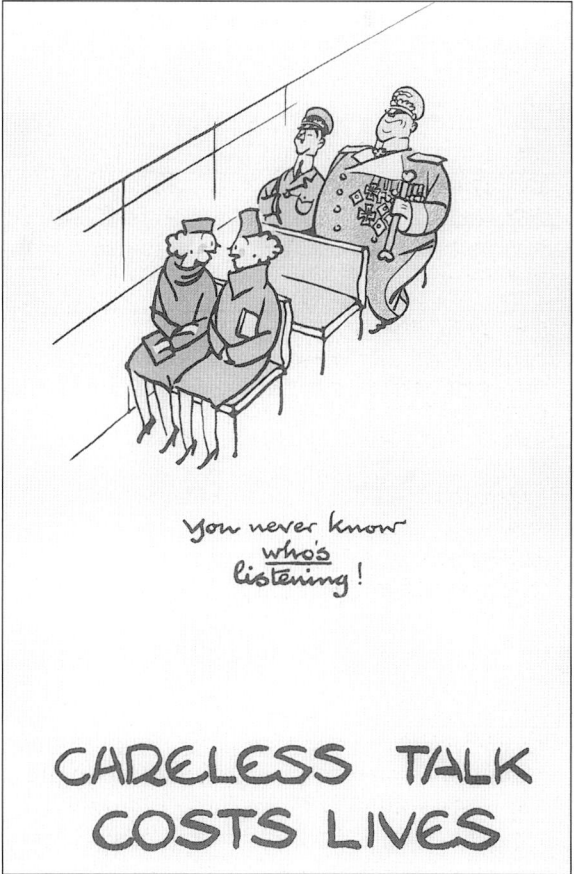

_____

_____

_____

_____

_____

You never know
who's
listening!

CARELESS TALK
COSTS LIVES

Evacuation

- Read this extract from the diary of a 12-year-old girl.

> It was on June 14th 1940 that I left London. I did not know exactly where I was going. But I did know that we were going a very long way. We left Paddington about nine thirty a.m. Some of the very small children were crying. The children numbered about a hundred and eleven, including a number of teachers, helpers and Red Cross nurses. When the train left Paddington Station, the children brightened up. They soon forgot their troubles, and they were all looking out of the carriage window, talking and laughing for all they were worth.

- Explain what is happening.

_____

_____

_____

_____

_____

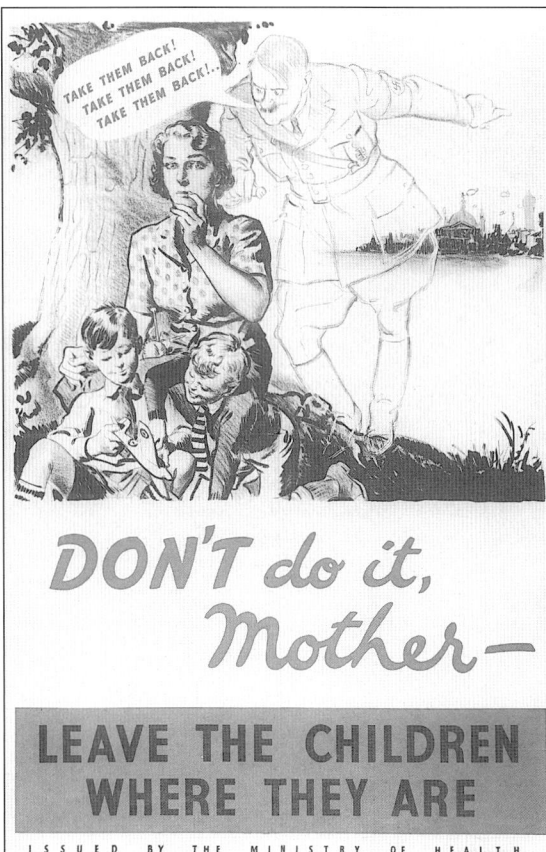

TAKE THEM BACK!
TAKE THEM BACK!
TAKE THEM BACK!..

DON'T do it, mother—

LEAVE THE CHILDREN WHERE THEY ARE

ISSUED BY THE MINISTRY OF HEALTH

- Explain this poster.

_____

_____

_____

_____

_____

_____

_____

_____

_____

FOLENS HISTORY IN ACTION 4 © Folens (copiable page)

Protecting Britain from the enemy

● Complete the table to show three ways that the government used to protect Britain.

Picture			
What people did			Street lamps extinguished and signposts removed.
Reason			
How it affected people			It was hard to find your way in an area you didn't know.

Children should:
- know that British cities were subjected to prolonged bombing in World War Two.
- learn how people protected themselves from the bombs.
- understand the significance of the Battle of Britain in World War Two.

Background

Hitler knew that unless the RAF was destroyed an invading fleet would not be able to cross the channel. He sent the German air force to destroy British air bases and aircraft factories. In the summer of 1940 the RAF defeated the *Luftwaffe* watched from below by thousands of people in the south of England. In September 1940, Hitler changed tactics and began the bombing of British cities in an effort to damage the economy and cause panic and fear, thereby forcing surrender. This campaign, known as the Blitz, inflicted terrible damage. On the 10 and 11 May 1941, German bombers dropped 708 tons of bombs on London killing 1400 and injuring 1792. Emergency workers and volunteer helpers all worked to deal with the destruction. It was exhausting and many were left homeless as a result, but people adjusted, kept working and helped each other.

In London the underground stations were used as shelters during the air raids. Public shelters were built and families with gardens (27% of the population) could have an Anderson shelter. They were very small, flooded easily and did not keep out the noise of an air raid, but they could take six people and if correctly built would withstand anything but a direct hit. A hole in the ground, three or four feet deep, was dug. The corrugated steel pieces were bolted together making an arch six feet high. Then the rear section was put into place followed by the front in a similar fashion, leaving room for an entrance. The shelter was then covered with a thick layer of earth. People would cover the floor with cement or wood. Morrison shelters had a steel roof and wire mesh sides and were more convenient as they were used indoors.

Starting Points	Main Activity	Simplified Activity	Extension Activity
W7 *'The Battle of Britain'* Show the children photographs of German and British planes used in 1940. Explain why Hitler needed to destroy the RAF.	Read the newspaper report with the children. Ask them to discuss in pairs how it could be represented in a picture, before they begin to draw.	Ask the children to illustrate the most exciting part of the report in one picture.	Give the children a range of resources; ask them to find out more information about the Battle of Britain and report to the rest of the class.
W8 *'Air raids'* Explain the meaning of air raid. Show the children photographs of the damage done by bombs.	Look at the pictures with the children and use them to talk about what was supposed to happen after a raid. Then ask them to write the instructions.	Ask the children to write a description of what is happening for a few pictures only.	Ask the children to role-play the telephone calls from the warden to the control centre, and the control centre to the emergency services.
W9 *'Shelters'* Talk about the different sorts of shelter people used, showing photographs if possible.	Ask the children to discuss the picture in pairs and tell each other how the shelter was built. Ask some of them to report to you before everyone completes the activity.	Ask the children to draw the pieces of the shelter and how they think they would be put together.	Ask the children to make a table showing the advantages and disadvantages of different shelters.

Plenary

Continue building the museum display by collecting together photographs and pictures used for pages 69–71 and either constructing the text for an interpretive panel or preparing a talk for visitors.

The Battle of Britain

I was one of hundreds of Londoners who stood in the streets cheering as two bombers were sent hurtling to destruction by our fighters yesterday. Thousands of feet above us we watched a terrific battle as fighters and bombers dodged in and out of the clouds. In a clear patch of blue sky I watched a bomber roar along with a fighter hard on its tail. Machine guns rattled as the fighter swooped after it. For a few seconds we watched a thrilling air duel. Then the bomber almost stood on its nose in mid-air, came hurtling down in a death dive and blew up before it reached the ground. The pilot bailed out and we watched him slowly glide down.

● Draw a picture to show what the writer could see.

● Explain why this battle was so important.

_____

_____

_____

Air raids

- The government issued photographs to show what should happen in an air raid. Use the drawings and the words to write a list of instructions for the wardens and rescue workers.

①
warden
nearest post

②
telephone
control centre

③
control centre

stretcher parties

ambulance

fire-fighters

④
heavy rescue team
first casualties

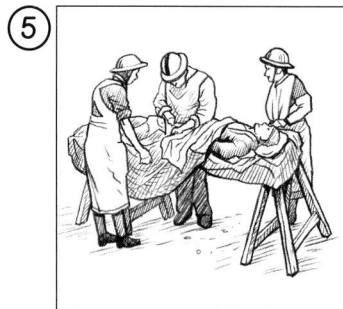

⑤
doctors and nurses
makeshift operating tables

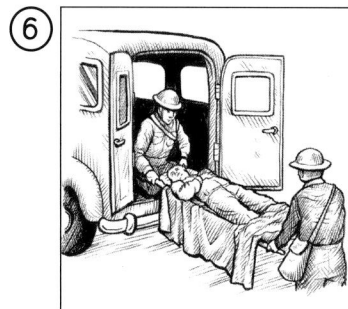

⑥
ambulance
hospital

Instructions

_____

_____

_____

_____

_____

_____

FOLENS HISTORY IN ACTION 4

Shelters

- Look at the drawing of people making an Anderson shelter.

- Label the illustration with these words:

pit	corrugated steel	bolts	earth	wood

- Write a description of how it is made.

_____

_____

_____

_____

_____

Children should:

- know that many foods and goods were in short supply during World War Two.
- understand some of the measures that were introduced to share and increase supplies.

Background

In 1939, 60% of food in Britain was imported. Supplies became more and more limited during the war, as cargo ships were either sunk or used for other purposes. Food rations were introduced in January 1940; they varied throughout the war and continued after 1945. Ration books contained coupons to be exchanged for basic items; an additional 16 coupons could be exchanged for any item. Everyone was encouraged to grow their own vegetables; back gardens were dug up and every available area converted to allotments. People kept chickens and rabbits and even shared a pig. More land was given over to farming and farmers were advised on production methods. The Women's Land Army replaced the male labour force on farms.

Clothes were rationed from 1 June 1941; 66 coupons per year at first, later reduced to 48, including sheets and towels. A man's shirt was 5 coupons, a jacket 13 coupons, and a tie 1 coupon. The design of clothes (and other goods) became very simple, to save on material. By 1942 paper was in short supply; envelopes were reused many times. Glass and valves for radios were scarce; petrol was not allowed for private cars; people were encouraged to 'make do and mend'; boys collected waste materials, which could be recycled. It was considered that, as well as reducing demand, salvage would help people to feel that they were making a contribution to the war effort and so boost morale.

Starting Points	Main Activity	Simplified Activity	Extension Activity
W10 *'Food rations'* Show children a photograph of a ration book. Explain what it was for.	Ask the children to read and discuss the sentences in pairs. Encourage them to work out or guess the correct choice. Discuss each sentence as a class and ask them to then underline the correct choice.	Ask the children to work with a partner who can help to read and understand the statements and discuss them.	Ask the children to write a sentence for each picture giving a brief description of the wartime measure that was adopted.
W11 *'Feed the family'* Show and weigh out samples of the items for the adult ration on page 74.	Ask the children to work in groups of four. Make sure that each group has a child who can act as note-taker. Tell each group if they have a garden or an allotment. Allocate family roles (optional). Discuss the tasks involved in growing vegetables and keeping animals. Give the class a time limit to reach an agreement.		
W12 *'Salvage'* Talk about the reasons for salvaging materials in the war, and how it would help people to feel that they were doing something useful.	Ask the children to talk about the posters in pairs before writing an explanation and designing their own poster.	Ask the children to write a sentence about each picture and, if necessary, give them some suggestions for the design of their own poster.	The day before the lesson, ask the children to bring in some unwanted items of clothing from home. After they have finished the main activity, ask the children to go through the clothes and decide how they would 'make do and mend'.

Plenary

Complete the museum display by collecting together photographs and pictures used for pages 73–75 and either constructing the text for an interpretive panel or preparing a talk for visitors.

Food rations

• Underline the words to make correct sentences.

In 1939 most food in Britain came from **abroad/British farms**.

German submarines sank many British cargo ships, so there was **less/more** food.

The government was worried that the price of food would go **down/up**.

Food rations were introduced so that **everybody/nobody** would get a fair share.

All foods/Not all foods were rationed.

Bacon, butter and sugar were some of the **last/first** things to be rationed.

Bread **was/was not** rationed.

Some foods, like **apples/bananas**, were just not available.

People were **less/more** healthy when food was rationed.

• Write a sentence for each picture describing the wartime measure.

Feed the family

Role-play

You are part of a family (two children and two adults) in May 1941.

Here are the weekly food rations for an adult (shown in modern units of measure).
These quantities varied during the war, depending on their availability.

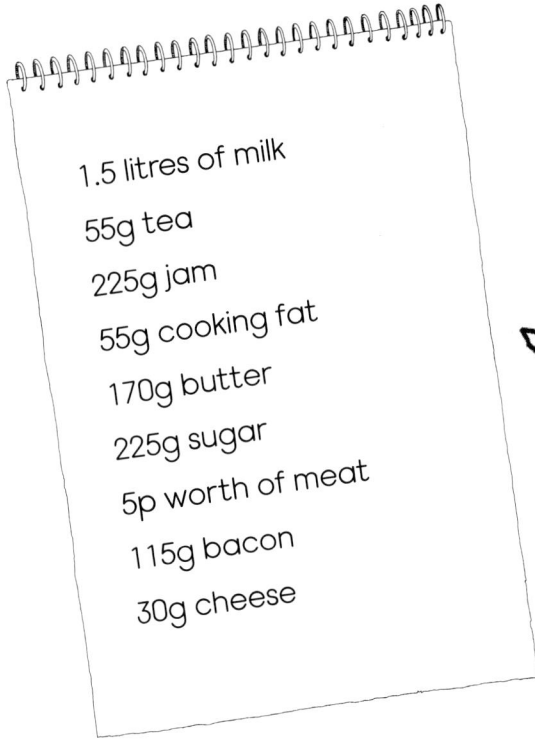

1.5 litres of milk

55g tea

225g jam

55g cooking fat

170g butter

225g sugar

5p worth of meat

115g bacon

30g cheese

Decide the following:

■ where you will grow vegetables and what you will grow

■ whether to keep any animals and how you will feed them

■ who is going to do all the jobs?

● Write down what you have agreed.

_____

_____

_____

_____

_____

Salvage

- Look at the two government posters.

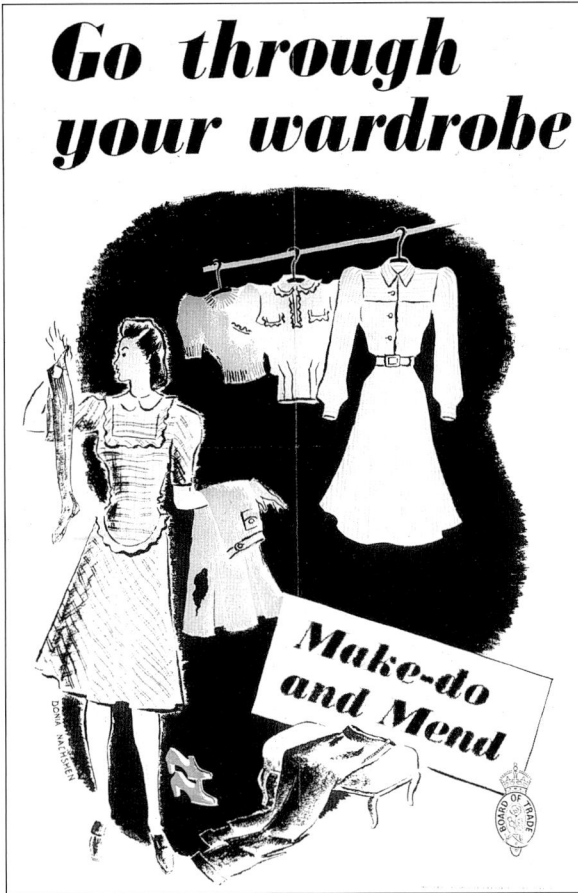

Go through your wardrobe

Make-do and Mend

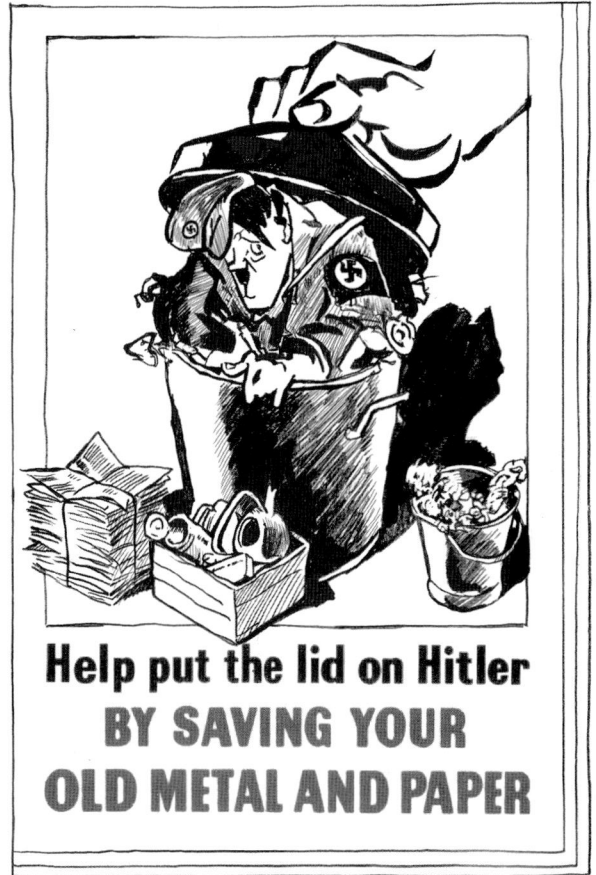

Help put the lid on Hitler
BY SAVING YOUR
OLD METAL AND PAPER

- Explain what each poster is telling people to do and why.

_____

_____

_____

_____

_____

_____

_____

_____

- Design a poster to encourage people in the war to save glass.

Children should:

- recognise diaries and living memory as ways of learning about World War Two.
- know that Jews were persecuted under Hitler.
- consolidate new vocabulary related to World War Two.

Background

After the Soviet Union had joined the Allies (May 1941), followed by the United States (December 1941), Hitler's expansion was halted. On 6 and 7 June 1944 the Allies landed in France. On 7 May 1945 the Nazis surrendered and 8 May is Victory in Europe day; the defeat of Japan came soon after.

Anne Frank (1929–44) began her diary in 1942. It gives a detailed account, from a teenage perspective, of her family going into hiding and daily life under such difficult circumstances. In it she wrote, 'I want to go on living even after my death! And therefore I am grateful to God for giving me this gift of expressing all that is in me.'

The memories of life as a young child in World War Two are contributed by Cynthia Montreal (1935–), now a grandmother. She lived in Edgbaston, near Birmingham.

Starting Points	Main Activity	Simplified Activity	Extension Activity
W13 *'Anne Frank'* Talk about the importance of diaries as a way of learning about ordinary people. Show a copy of Anne Frank's diary and read an extract.	Read the paragraphs with the children. Ask them to work in pairs and agree on the sequence. Remind them to use dates and ages as clues. Ask some of the children to report back to you before they stick the paragraphs. Read the text again together.	Give the children a list of key words about Anne and ask them to use the words to write sentences about her.	Give the children copies of the diary, or a chapter of the diary. After they have finished the main activity, ask them to read a section and tell the class about it.
W14 and **W15** *'Memories of the war (1) and (2)'* Explain the term 'within living memory' and discuss the importance of recording people's memories of significant events.	**W14** *'Memories of the war (1)'* Read the text with the children. Discuss their reactions to these childhood experiences of the war. Ask them to prepare questions for their own interviews with neighbours or family members who lived through the war. Alternatively, invite two visitors to the next lesson to answer the children's questions.		
	W15 *'Memories of the war (2)'* Ask the children to record their interview by writing 'in the voice of' the interviewee.	Ask the children to record the interview and leave them to choose first or third person.	After they have completed the main activity, ask the children to look for and record common features of the three people's memories.
W16 *'War words'*	Photocopy the sheet on to card. Revise the meanings of the words on page 80. The game could be played in pairs, or groups of three or four. It will probably work best if children of mixed reading ability are grouped together.		

Plenary

Recap on all that the children have learned about World War Two by asking them to imagine that they are in the year 1944. Ask them to say all of the ways in which their lives would be different from now.

Anne Frank

● Cut out these paragraphs about Anne Frank and put them in the correct order.

A.

Anne was four years old when Hitler came to power in 1934. He made laws against Jewish people. They had to wear stars on their clothes and were not allowed in theatres or cinemas. Anne's family moved to Amsterdam to be safe from Hitler. Anne had a normal, happy life. She liked reading and music and she talked a lot!

B.

On 6 June 1944 they heard on a secret radio that the Allies had landed in France. Hitler was losing, but Anne didn't live to see the war end. Somebody had told the Gestapo and they were raided on 4 August. They were sent on the last train that went to the concentration camps. Edith died of starvation. Anne and Margot were sent to another camp where they caught typhus. Margot died, followed a few days later by Anne.

C.

Anne Frank was born in 1929 in Frankfurt, Germany. She belonged to a Jewish family who had lived in Frankfurt for hundreds of years. Her parents were Otto and Edith. She had one older sister called Margot.

D.

When Margot was ordered to report to a concentration camp, Otto Frank decided to take the family into hiding. They could not pack any bags because the Gestapo (German police) would suspect something, so they just put on lots of clothes and took a few things each. They hid in rooms at the top of the building where Otto worked. The doorway was hidden by a bookcase.

E.

Another family joined them, so there were eight people living together all the time in a small space. They had to be silent all day. Some Dutch friends brought food for them but sometimes there was not enough. Anne wrote in her diary every day.

F.

Otto was the only one of the family to survive. A friend of his had found Anne's diary on the floor of the hiding place and she persuaded him to get it published. He did, and since 1947 more than 20 million copies of Anne's diary have been sold.

G.

Eight months after the start of World War Two, Hitler's army invaded the Netherlands. Anne's parents wanted to take the family to England but they were not allowed to.

Memories of the war (1)

Cynthia Montreal was four years old when the war began. These are some of the things she remembers.

Cynthia at 4

When the bombs started my sister and I were evacuated to Overbury in Worcestershire. I remember feeling completely alone. I woke up in the night and cried a lot and my mother came to collect us both. We all stayed in Worcester for a while in two rooms with a shared kitchen.

When we returned home bombs had dropped on our street and the foundations of the house had been shaken, but it was still there. My parents had dug up the back garden to grow vegetables and we had some chickens.

We all had to carry gas masks in cardboard boxes worn round our necks. In school we had to practise putting them on. They were horrible and rubbery with a little piece of glass to see out of. We had to sing or recite poetry wearing them. I felt as if I was suffocating.

There were no sweets except for the occasional soft jammy one that I thought was horrid. I remember egg powder and eating boiled potatoes with one egg stirred in. There was no toilet paper and we had to cut up newspaper, or whatever we could get. We were short of bed linen. The house leaked because there were no men available for repair work.

There were more air raids. When the siren sounded we sat in the hall so that if the bombs started we could go in the cellar. I had a horror of going in the cellar because it was cold and damp. Sometimes we spent the whole night in the hall. Once I was caught in an air raid on the way to school. Somebody took me down into a bare concrete room and I felt very lost amongst all the strangers.

My father was too old to be called up so he was an air-raid warden; he had to go out and check there were no lights showing through curtains in the street. I was always glad when he came back.

It always seemed to be cold and dark. We lived in one room most of the time. Coal was rationed and when people lit bonfires on VE day and used coal, my mother was rather disapproving. All through my teenage years the shops stayed quite empty and when I started nursing at the age of 18, butter and sugar were still rationed.

Memories of the war (2)

- Write your questions for your interview here:

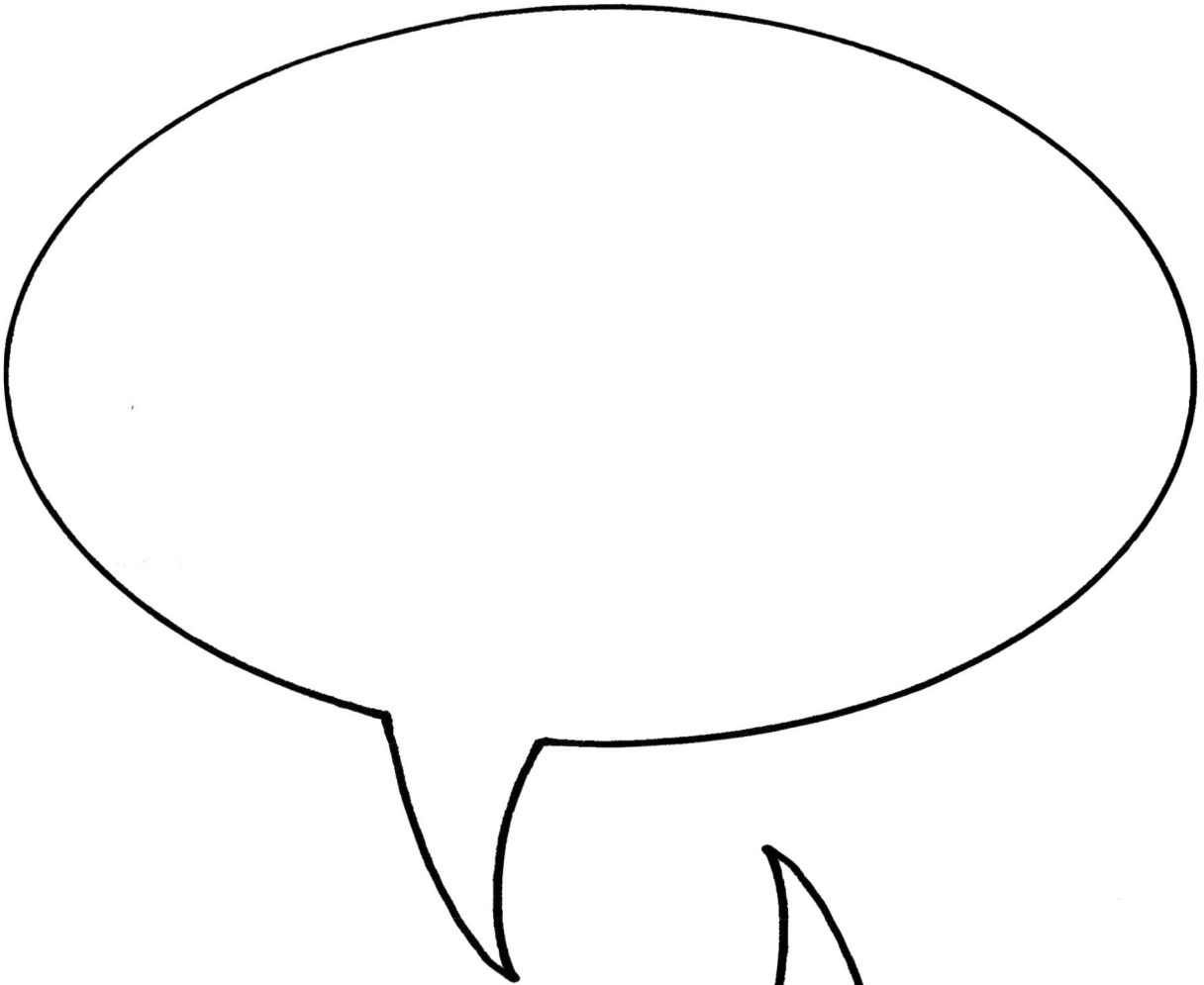

- Write the answers here:

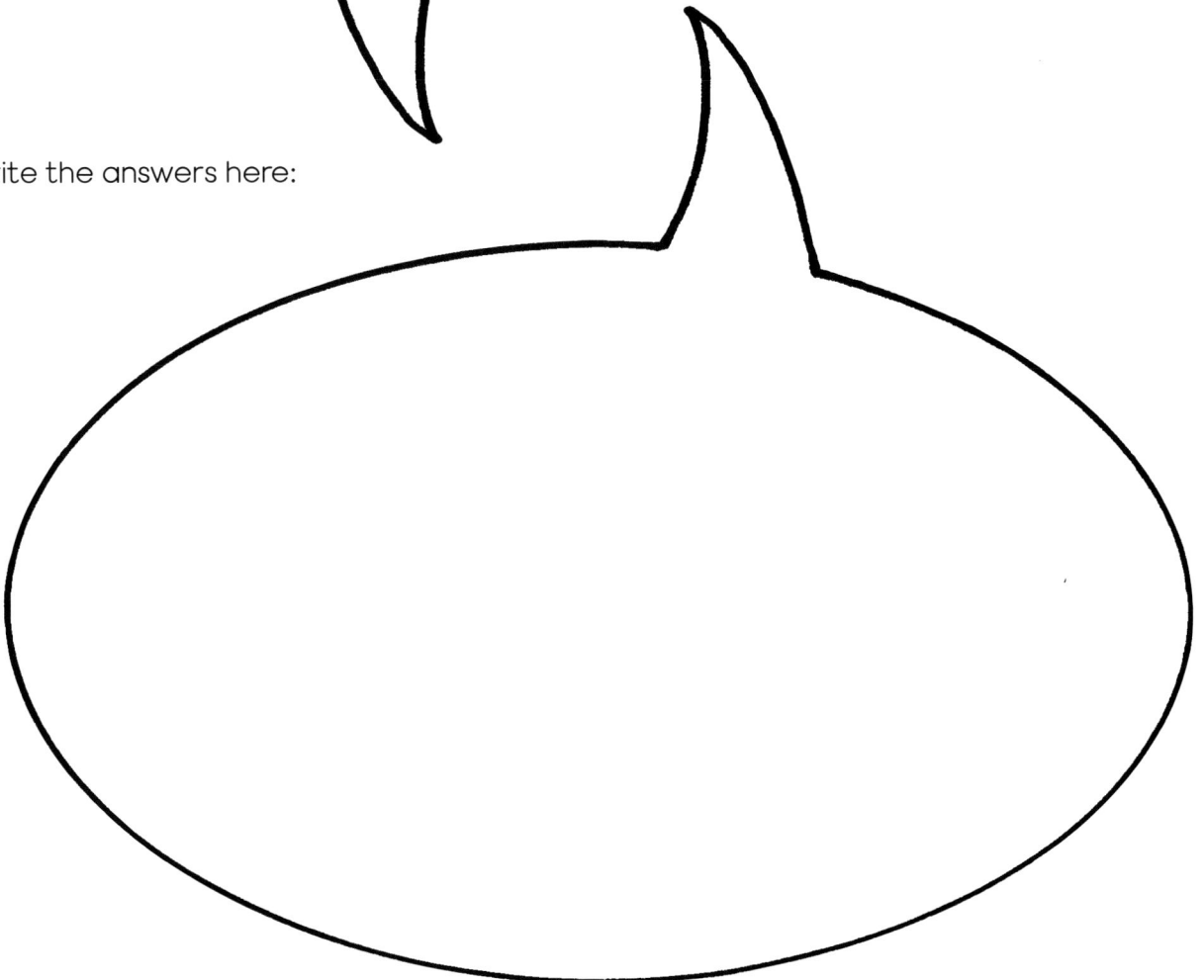

War words

Cut out the cards, shuffle them and spread them out on the table, face down. Take it in turns to turn over two cards. If you have a matching word and meaning, keep them. If not, turn them over again. The winner is the person who has collected the most cards at the end of the game.

Allies	evacuation	Anderson shelter	VE day
Axis powers	air raid	siren	blackout
the Blitz	rationing	coupons	
internee	RAF	salvage	

A way of sharing out limited supplies of food.	A small building that could protect a family from bombs.	The period of heavy bombing on London.	A person who was held in a camp in case they helped the enemy.	An attack from the sky by bombers.
The countries that fought alongside Germany in World War Two.	The countries that fought alongside Britain in World War Two.	Royal Air Force – the British fighter planes.	Letting no light show outside at night.	Sending people (mainly children) away from a dangerous area.
Pieces of paper that could be exchanged for food or clothes.	The warning noise that sounded when enemy planes were coming.	The end of the war – Victory in Europe day.	Collecting and recycling of materials like metal or paper.	

FOLENS HISTORY IN ACTION 4